ECONOMIC GROWTH IN CANADA

CANADIAN STUDIES IN ECONOMICS

A series of studies now edited by Douglas G. Hartle, sponsored by the Social Science Research Council of Canada, and published with financial assistance from the Canada Council

Economic Growth in Canada

A QUANTITATIVE ANALYSIS

SECOND EDITION

N. H. Lithwick

UNIVERSITY OF TORONTO PRESS

TO YVONNE
ALEXANDER, DAHLIA, AND HILLEL

PREFACE

SUBSEQUENT TO THE FIRST EDITION of this volume I attempted to use some of the analytical tools developed herein to explore two related questions: the so-called gap in income levels between Canada and the United States, and the relatively poorer Canadian productivity performance over the period 1956–66. The former involved the application of time-series instruments cross-sectionally, while the latter surveyed developments in a period subsequent to that covered by the first edition. This was published by the Canadian Trade Committee of the Private Planning Association of Canada in 1967 under the title: *Prices, Productivity, and Canada's Competitive Position.*

When the University of Toronto Press proposed a second printing of *Economic Growth in Canada,* I suggested that this study would be highly complementary through extending the analytical scope and the coverage in time of the original study. I should like to convey my gratitude to the Private Planning Association of Canada for assisting in the initial publication and in so graciously consenting to having it included as Chapter Seven of this volume.

My greatest debt is to Professor Simon Kuznets who directed the doctoral dissertation which formed the basis of the original study. In addition I have received useful criticism from Professors Richard Caves and Thomas A. Wilson, Dr. William Hood and Mr. Gordon Garston. The new Chapter Seven has benefitted greatly from comments by my colleagues Professors Thomas K. Rymes and H. E. English and from Dr. Tom Powrie of the Private Planning Association of Canada.

This work was initially published with the help of a grant from the Social Science Research Council, using funds provided by the Canada Council.

CONTENTS

TABLES

ECONOMIC GROWTH IN CANADA

CHAPTER ONE

INTRODUCTION

THE NATURE and the determinants of economic growth can best be comprehended by examining the process in the countries that have been succesful in attaining a steadily increasing, high level of economic activity.

The fact that so few countries have managed to become developed, and that for those which have, very incomplete records of their progress exist, make our knowledge of economic growth rather limited. As we shall show, Canada has undergone such an evolution, and relatively abundant statistical descriptions of this process are available. Unfortunately, these data are still in a very primitive state so that little analysis has been undertaken. This is surprising, because the gains from adding the experience of another country to our meagre stock of knowledge in this field appear to be substantial.

The hope that further study of economic growth in Canada would serve the purpose of enlarging our understanding of growth in general, and would lead to an appreciation of the specific features in Canada's development has been the motivating factor underlying this study.

The theoretical model that forms the basis of subsequent analysis is the now familiar Cobb-Douglas function.[1] Our procedure will be to apply this model, incorporating several refinements which permit an evaluation of labour's changing quality, to Canada's economic growth over as long a period as possible. In Chapters One and Two, this analysis is undertaken for the total Canadian economy for the period 1926-56. The findings are compared to those for the United States and several interesting differences emerge. In the United States, the improvement in the quality of labour has led to a higher growth rate of labour input than has been the case in Canada. This is due largely to the much greater relative success the United States has had in educating its population. On the other hand, Canada has devoted more resources to fixed capital formation so that the growth rate of this factor has been higher than in the United States. When these two measured inputs are weighted together, their combined growth rate is quite similar for the two countries. Since Canada's output has grown at a substantially higher rate than has that of the United States over these thirty years, the initial implication is that productivity advance—defined as a residual in this model—has grown much faster in Canada.

One possible source of this discrepancy, however, forces us to amend this premature conclusion. In Chapters Three and Four we apply the same model to sectoral growth, and find that at this dis-aggregated level, the growth rate of productivity in comparable industries is very similar for the two countries. It is obvious, therefore, that the source of the discrepancy in the aggregate productivity measures is the interaction between industries in the course of growth, and we call this the "inter-industry shift" in the structure of production. Devising several measures of this process, we find that the residuals net of this factor grow at quite similar rates in the two countries, as we would expect from the parallelism that was found at the sectoral level. Further dis-aggregation of the manufacturing sector, to remove interaction within that sector, contributed marginally to still closer reconciliation.

To place these findings into a longer perspective, we examine growth in the two countries from 1890 in Chapter Five. In addition, Norway's growth is studied to provide what is perhaps a more reasonable basis for comparing Canada's performance. The results of this chapter suggest common patterns of growth in the three countries, including a decelerating growth rate of labour input, and a sharp increase in the residual's growth rate over time.

No further attempt was made to explain the remaining residual growth rate, as did Denison. This is due to our uneasiness with many of his refinements, and the particularly great weakness of using a model embodying an assumption of constant returns to scale. For any returns to scale will be hidden in our residual. Similarly, further aspects of quality change, such as on-the-job training and the improved quality of new capital, are contained in our residual. Much more theoretical as well as empirical research into these factors is required before the true rate of technological advance can be determined using this residual procedure.

Our main conclusion from this study is that modern economic growth has been very similar in Canada and the United States. The main differences in the aggregative growth rates can be attributed to the earlier decline of agriculture in the United States as compared to the very sharp, recent contraction of that sector in Canada. The reasons for this parallel development in the two countries have no doubt been the very great mobility of men, capital, and technology between them, together with the increasing similarity in the tastes of their people.

This growing homogeneity of the economies has appeared to some Canadians to be a threat to the "national identity" of this country. To offset this, protection has been maintained, along with ownership-of-industry and similar gimmicks. Whether these measures will lead to a peculiarly Canadian type of growth is highly unlikely, given the similarities in tastes and technology, and the high degree of factor mobility. These doubtful benefits should be weighed very carefully against the cost, calculated in terms of lower real income, that Canadians are now paying for these policies. An integrated North American economy will maximize income in both countries and our reading of the past suggests that attempts to delay it have but one result; that is, to impose a fruitless burden on Canadians.

The lack of sufficiently detailed data for Canada has necessitated a great number of estimates, including capital stock data by industry back to 1937, and by major components back to 1926. In addition, quality adjustments for the labour series were required, along with calculations of inter-industry shifts. To improve readability they have been relegated to the appendices.

CHAPTER TWO

A MODEL OF ECONOMIC GROWTH

FACED WITH CRUDE DATA and with models which present many problems, we decided to employ a familiar model which can incorporate these data in a straightforward manner. This is the Cobb-Douglas function,

$$Y = A \, L^a \, K^b,$$

where Y is the measure of output, L is the size of the labour input, K is the capital input, and A is the residual.[1] This may be transformed so that the variables are considered in terms of their respective growth rates, as indicated by the bars over the relevant symbols,

$$\overline{Y} = \overline{A} + a \, \overline{L} + b \, \overline{K}.$$

The coefficients "a" and "b" will not be estimated statistically, but will be derived from the particular variable's share in national income. The increase of the measured factors—labour and capital—weighted by these coefficients indicates what magnitude output would have attained if no other elements entered to influence it. The divergence between the observed growth and this theoretical one is ascribed to the growth of the residual, or, as denoted earlier, to productivity advance.

Early studies tended to consider labour and capital inputs in their simplest terms, leaving all else within the residual. A more recent study[2] attempted a decomposition of this residual to a greater extent. In essence, this is accomplished by allocating to the various factors of production changes in their quality as well as in their quantity. Denison includes in his labour series the effects of changes in age and sex composition, of reduced hours of work as they affect labour efficiency, and of increased formal education of the labour force. In addition, such elements as the advance of knowledge, market impediments, and economies of scale are separated from the residual. These procedures will be followed in this study where they are considered to be theoretically valid.

In evaluating this model, it is useful to consider its implicit assumptions. One is that the relative earnings of the measured factors are fixed at base period proportions. Since these earnings are assumed to be proportional to the marginal productivities of the factors, it follows that the marginal rates of substitution between all factors are also fixed for the entire period. Thus, shifts in the marginal rate of substitution because of non-neutral technological change or differences in factor availabilities are precluded. The selection of a base period is consequently a task requiring great care. While it is recognized that these assumptions are rigid, the model has the offsetting advantage of being able to show in an explicit fashion how the elements, generally accepted to be of economic significance, enter into the development process.

A more practical problem must be faced when attention turns to the measurement of growth. This is the selection of the period to be studied so as to avoid a possible bias that might arise from comparing different phases of cyclical disturbances, be they of short period or of the longer swings, in the various economic time series. With the data that are available for Canada, it is impossible to fulfil this requirement for the longer swings as we cannot extend the analysis prior to the 1920s. However, corrections can be made for the shorter "business" cycle. It is assumed that the degree of unemployment of the labour force indicates the phase at which the short cycle of output stands. Thus, three per cent unemployment at two dates indicates that, barring unusual circumstances, the economy was at the same distance from full employment of its resources in these years, and that they are therefore directly comparable. Implicit in this assumption is a coincidence in the cyclical behaviour of inputs with that of output. Otherwise, while output in two years may be on the same trend line, one or more of the inputs may not be on their trend lines, so that the comparison of these inputs to determine their trend growth rate is not valid. This sort of problem could arise if changes in the time relationships occurred as a result of certain irregular influences, or a lengthening of the period of production.

With these requirements in mind, and with the desire to obtain as long a period of time as possible, we have chosen the years 1926 through 1956 as the observation points for our study of potential economic growth in Canada. The extent of unemployment in the labour force was 3.0 per cent in the former year and 3.1 per cent in 1956.[3] In addition, these years were normal in most respects, in contrast to the turbulent war and early post-war years.

During this period, real Gross National Expenditure (GNE) in prices of 1949 grew at an average annual rate of 3.89 per cent. It is possible to test this rate by looking at the rate between other comparable periods. Thus, from 1921 to 1959, with unemployment higher but comparable at 5.8 per cent and 5.6 per cent respectively, GNE grew at 3.92 per cent annually. Similarly, for 1922 to 1957, for which unemployment was 4.6 and 4.3 per cent, the rate of growth was 3.91 per cent. If periods of more than one year are selected as the terminal dates, similar growth rates are observed. Between 1924-6 and 1955-7, the rate was 3.88 per cent, and unemployment averaged 4.1 per cent in the first period and 3.8 per cent in the second. It appears that the growth rate for our selected dates does come very close to a potential or trend rate, as far as the latter exists within longer cycles of economic activity.[4]

While these results indicate that our selection of 1926 and 1956 is reasonable for measuring the trend in the growth of output, we must examine the pattern of input cycles to see if the years are also reasonable for the consideration of trends in our input measures. Plotting the annual series of the key inputs, including the labour force, man-hours, and capital stock of the various types, against GNE indicates great similarity in their cyclical behaviour. The year 1926 is on the upswing of all the series which terminates with the peak in 1929 or shortly thereafter. Also, 1956 is on the upswing of all series, beginning with the trough of 1954 and reaching a peak in 1956 or 1957. Thus, we may conclude that the selected years do give us trend rates of output growth, and do not introduce serious bias into our input measures which are all in the same phase of the cycle as is output.

To conclude this chapter, we compare the growth rate of Canada with that of the United States. In addition to the growth of total product, several alternative measures of economic growth are included (Table 1).

It is clear that whatever measure of growth is used, the rate of growth in Canada was significantly above that in the United States. A good part of the following analysis will be devoted to explaining this difference, for underlying it is the particularly interesting question of how growth occurs under varied economic circumstances.

TABLE 1

COMPARATIVE ECONOMIC GROWTH, CANADA AND US
(percentages)

Measure of growth *	Average annual growth rate	
	Canada (1926-56)	US (1929-57)
GNP	3.89	2.93
GNP per person employed	2.37	1.60
GNP per capita	2.01	1.69

* Prices of 1949 for Canada, and 1954 for US.
SOURCES: Canada; DBS, *National Accounts*, Table 5 for GNP and Table 3 below for remainder. US; Denison, *Economic Growth in the United States*, 21, Table 3.

One possible source of bias in these comparisons of growth rates is the use of different base years for the United States and Canada. For series in 1947 prices, the growth rate of GNP in the United States was 3.01 per cent in contrast to the slightly lower rate of 2.93 per cent with 1954 prices.[5] This indicates that there is a slight amount of distortion downwards, but that the extent is not significant, and our conclusions are not affected as a result.

CHAPTER THREE

ECONOMIC GROWTH IN CANADA, 1926-56

I. LABOUR AND ITS GROWTH

BETWEEN 1926 AND 1956, the population of Canada almost doubled, rising from 9,451,000 to 16,081,000,[1] which implies an average annual growth rate of 1.78 per cent.[2] The proportion of the population serving in the labour force is given by the participation rate, which has declined somewhat for Canada from 57.8 to 53.8 per cent over the period.[3] This is in contrast to the United States case where the participation rate showed a slight increase from 56.2 to 58.0 per cent.[4]

A closer examination of the performance within the various age and sex groups may indicate some of the reasons for the different behaviour of the participation rates. Sufficiently detailed data are available for Canada since 1946 when the Labour Force Survey began. Even in this restricted span of time the key factors leading to the differences can be detected.

TABLE 2

PARTICIPATION RATES BY AGE AND SEX, CANADA AND US, 1946-56
(percentages)

Ages	1946		1956	
Canada				
	Males	Females	Males	Females
14-19	60.4	37.8	48.1	33.9
20-24	88.8	48.1	91.7	47.1
25-44	97.0	23.2	97.6	24.5
45-64	93.4	15.3	92.0	20.8
over 65	47.5	5.0	34.1	4.5
United States				
14-19	53.5	32.1	50.9	31.7
20-24	81.0	46.2	89.5	46.2
25-44	94.3	34.3	96.4	38.9
45-64	92.0	27.9	91.5	40.4
over 65	47.4	8.3	39.1	10.6

SOURCES: Canada; from Labour Force Survey, as given for 1946 in Hood and Scott, *Output, Labour and Capital*, 184, Table 4.21, and for 1956 in Senate of Canada, Special Committee on Manpower and Employment, *Proceedings*, no. 1 (Nov. 1960), 41, Table J. United States; *Historical Statistics*, Series D 13-25, 71.

Table 2 indicates that the trend in Canada's male participation rate has been roughly similar to that of the United States, with a greater decrease, however, in the youngest and oldest groups. The former decrease is explained by the delay, in Canada, in educating as many of its young men in comparison to the United

States in the early period, and its subsequent catching-up, to which we shall return in our discussion of the role of education. The causes of the lower participation rate for men over sixty-five are not so clear, but the universal old-age pension scheme in Canada may be significant in this connection. Also, Canada has lately seen the decline of agriculture which has traditionally been a relatively large user of older workers.

The participation rate for females in Canada moved in ways different from that of females in the United States. In the case of the latter, there has been either stability or an increase in the participation rates for all age groups while, in Canada, the pattern has been the opposite, with an increase in the forty-five to sixty-four group, but stability or decline in all others. For the youngest group, education may again be the main factor. The childbearing age groups are critical in the comparison, for here the level of the participation rate as well as its change are distinctly different. It seems that there is a much lower propensity for young wives to work in Canada, in part because of the higher birth rate, which in turn receives at least some impetus from the family allowance payments of the federal government. Finally, the different pattern for females over sixty-five may again be a result of the decline of agriculture, and perhaps of the old-age pension scheme as well.

It appears, therefore, that the lower participation rate in Canada has in some measure been the result of government policies in the field of education as well as in welfare. Consequently, the labour force has grown less than it might have without these policies and the potential growth rate of output has been reduced thereby. The exact extent of this reduction cannot be estimated until some evaluation of the influence of these government programmes on the participation rates is made. These differential trends in participation have led to a rate of growth of the Canadian labour force lower than that of the population, whereas in the United States it was higher.[5]

The result of this divergence is, of course, a much higher dependency rate in Canada. In otherwords, the growth of the non-productive population has surpassed that of the labour force, whereas in the United States the opposite is the case. Therefore, although the gap in GNP per person employed in the two countries has been reduced by about 5½ per cent over this period, that of GNP per capita has been reduced only 2½ per cent, explaining the commonly observed relative stability in the latter ratio.

These rates are summarized in Table 3.

TABLE 3

GROWTH OF THE POPULATION AND THE LABOUR FORCE,
CANADA AND US
(percentages)

	Average annual rate of growth	
	Population	Labour force
Canada (1926-56)	1.78	1.54
United States (1929-57)	1.23	1.31

SOURCES: DBS, *Canadian Statistical Review*, 1959 Supplement, Tables 4 and 8; US Dept. of Commerce, *Historical Statistics of the US*, Series D1-12.

The growth of the labour force does not in itself measure the increase in labour input. In all sectors of the economy the length of the work day has decreased, and it is therefore necessary to consider the course of man-hours over this period.

From Appendix Table A-8 we calculate that aggregate man-hours increased at an average annual rate of 0.73 per cent. Denison attempts to refine his man-hour series further, in the belief that a reduction of average hours does not necessarily lead to a directly proportional decline in effective labour input. He contends that as the length of the work week has been reduced, employees have been both willing and able to work harder each hour they have remained on the job.

In his review of Denison's book, Abramovitz recognizes the historical association between shorter hours and greater intensity of work, but questions what he feels to be Denison's implied causal structure, that it is the reduction of hours which has led to increased effort.[6] He depicts a reverse situation, and one that is indeed typical, wherein the marginal productivity of labour is raised by means of a managerial innovation, part of which gain is subsequently taken by the worker in the form of leisure.

Both of these arguments are valid, but neither taken by itself is sufficiently realistic. It is the interaction of the two that is most typical. To show this, we employ the usual diagrammatical representation of the choice between income and leisure.

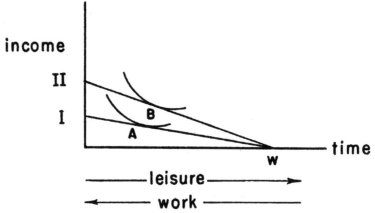

Fig. 1   The choice between income and leisure.

The traditional analysis parallels Abramovitz' reasoning, where an innovation raises the marginal productivity of labour, thereby shifting the wage line (the slope of which measures the wage rate) upward to W–II and equilibrium is re-established at B with part of the gain taken in the form of increased leisure (the horizontal distance between A and B) and part in increased income (the vertical distance between A and B). Denison introduces his feedback mechanism here, for as the worker reduces his hours of work, his own productivity while at work is altered thereby, and the wage line shifts once more, with a new equilibrium being established.

Thus, while it is possible to obtain a functional relationship between the decline in hours and productivity advance, this relationship does not indicate the nature of the underlying causal structure. If we could isolate these two effects, then Denison's refinement would be a welcome addition to our analysis of hours of labour input. However, the continuous interaction of the two effects renders this isolation statistically intractable. Even if we could isolate them, the estimation of the coefficients of the functional relationships would certainly require a more sophisticated technique than Denison's "best guess" method. These problems bar for the present an analysis along the lines proposed by Denison, and we therefore omit the whole problem of the consequence of hours reduction on labour efficiency.

Thus far in our analysis of the labour force and the growth of labour input, we have regarded each person employed as a homogeneous unit. Needless to say, there is infinite variety among the members of the labour force and it is necessary to standardize them for the main features leading to differential labour effectiveness. The two that we wish to deal with are age and sex differences, and the varying degrees of formal education possessed by members of the labour force.

A discussion of the procedures followed in estimating the effects of changes in age and sex is given in Appendix A-III. From Table A-21 we calculate that changes in the age and sex composition of the Canadian labour force led to a slight deterioration of its average quality of 3.23 per cent over the entire period of 1926–56. It is instructive to consider which segments of the labour force have undergone the most significant changes. Table 4 presents a summary description of these movements.

TABLE 4

CHANGING AGE AND SEX DISTRIBUTION OF THE CANADIAN LABOUR FORCE

Age	Labour force (thousands)				Percent increases	
	1921		1951		1921-51	
	Male	Female	Male	Female	Male	Female
Under 20	302.9	116.9	311.0	197.2	2.7	68.7
20-24	324.1	126.2	494.3	257.6	52.5	104.1
25-64	1930.9	234.2	3105.1	682.4	60.8	191.4
Over 65	125.2	12.7	212.4	27.2	69.7	114.2

SOURCE: See footnotes to Table A-9.

The fastest growing groups have been females over the age of twenty. Since women have a lower mean income than men of the same age, this rapid increase in the size of those groups with the lowest mean income implies that "adult males" have come to represent a declining proportion of the labour force. While the slackened rate of increase of men under twenty-five would tend to augment the average quality of the labour force, it has not been of sufficient magnitude to offset the rapid influx of women.

In the United States, the entry of women into the labour force has been very rapid also, but their earnings relative to the control group have been higher than that of their Canadian counterparts, indicating greater relative effectiveness with respect to adult males. This has led to a slight increase in the average quality of the United States labour force.[7]

A further adjustment that can be made to the labour factor takes into account the improvement in labour's effectiveness as a result of increased formal education.[8] Since we are using a marginal productivity analysis of factor returns, we must remove those elements entering into the income of the more highly educated which are not the direct result of education, but which derive from such phenomena as rare talent, subsidization of earned income by the return on inherited property, and other such sources of personal advantage which yield to the individual an economic rent.

That this component of income exists is recognized by most students of the role of education in growth, but adequate estimates of its magnitude are not available. Denison's approach is once more to make a best guess, which in this instance is to take the rent share as two-fifths of the reported income differentials. The same criticism which we offered in connection with his treatment of hours applies here, but with one exception; we feel that the theoretical foundation for some allowance is well established here, and this was not the case earlier. We therefore propose to use his suggested offset since it is the only one available, and because we wish to retain comparability between his estimates for the United States and ours for Canada.

The estimates in Appendix A-II indicate that the quality of the labour force in Canada improved by 6.85 per cent between 1926 and 1956 as a result of increased formal education. Denison estimates that in the United States this same factor contributed to a 14.2 per cent improvement in labour's quality between 1930 and 1960.[9] This is double the increase we get for Canada over a similar period and the disparity requires some explanation.

Perhaps the key element is the more extensive school programme in the United States, particularly in the early part of the twentieth century. This can be seen in Table 5.

TABLE 5

PROPORTION OF POPULATION UNDER 25 IN SCHOOL, CANADA AND US
(percentages)

	1891	1901	1911	1921	1931	1941	1951	1956
Canada	36.5	37.6	36.2	41.5	43.3	39.6	45.7	51.1
US	41.7	42.1	41.3	46.1	51.0	51.0	49.6	53.0

SOURCE: Census data of the two countries.

Canada appears to lag behind the United States, by about thirty years, in terms of extending education to the majority of its young people, and has only recently caught up because the proportion in the Unted States appears to have stabilized. It is to be expected therefore that the impact of education on growth in Canada will be smaller than in the United States in the period under consideration. In addition, we may expect that the increase in the quality of the Canadian labour force resulting from the closing of this gap will become significant in the late 1960s and thereafter.

One final methodological criticism of Denison's procedure in his evaluation of the role of education refers to his view that increasing by some factor the average number of days spent in school per year adds the same quantum to labour's effectiveness as does increasing the number of years of schooling by that same factor. In his review article[10] Abramovitz argues that it is difficult to believe that a person with a grade eight education in 1963 is as well educated as a college graduate in 1910. Nor does there appear to us to be any indication that the number of days of schooling has a direct effect on labour productivity as measured by earnings. Thus we conclude that Denison's refinement for days overstates by a substantial amount the contribution of education to economic growth, and this adjustment is therefore omitted from our subsequent analysis.

The effects of education on the growth of labour input in Canada are indicated in Table 6. In addition, we present the previous results for the other quality adjustments, and derive the total labour input with all these refinements included. The results are compared to Denison's for the United States, both as he estimates them, and as we have revised them to correspond to our Canadian data.

TABLE 6
LABOUR INPUT ADJUSTED FOR QUALITY, CANADA AND US
(percentages)

Component	Increase over entire period		
	Canada (1926-56)	US (1929-57)	
		Ours	Denison
Man-hours	24.5	17.48	35.0
Age and sex composition	—3.23	2.82	4.1
Education	6.85	13.21	29.6
Total labour input	28.73	36.75	82.1
Growth rate, labour input	0.84	1.12	2.16

SOURCE: Denison, *Economic Growth in the United States*, 85, Table 11.

The change in the United States estimates when Denison's questionable procedures are omitted is very large, mainly because of the two major refinements that we have held to be invalid; the adjustment for increasing effectiveness because of the decline in hours, and the role of increased days of schooling. It is possible to cite an independent study with regard to the contribution of education. This is Schultz' work on the return to education in which he estimates that the growth rate of educational capital in the labour force over the same period was 4.09 per cent.[11] Using his rate of income of 5.9 per cent on this capital, we calculate that the return to education accounted for about 11.5 per cent of national income in 1957. This would make the contribution of education to economic growth about 0.47 percentage points in the growth rate. Denison in his study allocates 0.67 percentage points of the growth rate to education, whereas our adjustment which omits days of schooling suggests a contribution by education of 0.48 percentage points. These results indicate that Denison's procedure overstates the role played by education, and that our refinement is of the correct order of magnitude.

The final adjustment involves the use of fixed weights for the age-sex changes in the distribution of the labour force, in contrast to Denison's changing weights. The small size of this item precludes any serious bias arising from this change, and permits comparability with the Canadian results.

Comparing the growth of labour input in the two countries, we find that man-hours increased somewhat less in the United States, largely because of the slower growth of its labour force. The fact that the quality of the labour force rose so much more than in Canada, both from changes in the age and sex composition and from very large gains from increased formal education, is the key to understanding the greater over-all growth of labour input in the United States. According to these findings, we cannot explain Canada's much higher growth rate by the labour factor. It is necessary therefore, to turn to the other measurable factor of production, capital, to see how it has entered into the process of economic growth in the two countries.

II. CAPITAL AND ITS GROWTH

Consideration of reproducible capital goods involves some rather lengthy estimation procedures, because of the lack of adequate capital stock data for the period we have chosen. There exists one sufficiently long series namely that of the Royal Commission on Canada's Economic Prospects,[12] covering the years 1926 through 1955. Unfortunately, this series has several limitations for our purposes, primarily because of lack of coverage but also because of some inconsistencies in the data.[13] As a result, we have undertaken to prepare new estimates of gross and net capital stock by type, for the period under consideration. These are described in detail in Appendix A-I.

TABLE 7
GROWTH RATES OF CAPITAL STOCK, CANADA AND US
(percentages)

Type of capital	Canada (1926-56)		US (1929-57)	
	Gross	Net	Gross	Net
Residential construction	2.77	2.55	1.46	1.40
Machinery & equipment	4.60	5.30	1.85	2.83
Business construction	2.21	1.63		0.56
Public structures	6.41	7.49	n.a.	3.46
Inventories	2.18	2.18	1.90	2.33
Investments abroad	3.50	3.50	1.97	1.97
Foreigners' investments within country	1.50	1.50	1.37	1.37
Total	2.50	2.21	1.88	1.61

SOURCES: Canada; Tables A-1 through A-4, A-6, and A-7. United States; Gross; Denison, *Economic Growth in the United States*, 100, Table 12. Net; Raymond W. Goldsmith, *The National Wealth of the United States in the Postwar Period*, NBER (Princeton, 1962), 119, Table A-6.

From the new data, we calculate the growth rates of the various types of capital. These are compared to similar data for the United States in Table 7. The findings suggest that the slower growth of labour input in Canada has been offset to some extent at least by a more rapid growth of all forms of capital than in the United States, measured on either a net or a gross basis. The source of this more rapid growth of capital in Canada is the higher and more rapidly growing capital formation proportions, as can be observed in Table 8.

It is unfortunate that the domestic ratios are not directly comparable between the two countries. Nevertheless, it is clear that the higher levels of capital formation in Canada were generated in large part by the high savings ratios on both a net and a gross basis.

TABLE 8
CAPITAL FORMATION PROPORTIONS, CANADA AND US
(percentages)

Ratio	Canada		US	
	1926-30	1952-58	1924-33	1946-55
Gross domestic capital formation/GDP	20.5	24.7	—	—
Net domestic capital formation/NDP	9.7	15.1	—	—
Gross national capital formation/GNP	19.4	22.5	18.4	21.9
Net national capital formation/NNP	7.9	12.4	7.5	9.0
Gross domestic capital formation/GNP	—	—	17.7	21.5
Net domestic capital formation/NNP	—	—	6.7	8.5

SOURCE: Simon Kuznets, "Quantitative Aspects of the Economic Growth of Nations," VI. "Long-Term Trends in Capital Formation Proportions," *Economic Development and Cultural Change*, IX, no. 4, part II (July 1961), 102, Table C-1, and 92, Table US-1.

III. THE ROLE OF NATURAL RESOURCES

Natural resources have figured very prominently in studies of Canada's economic growth. The now famous staple theory [14] claims that the key to development has been the exploitation of the country's plentiful resources to meet foreign demands in particular. The pattern emerges very early with the fur trade, then in turn with fishing and lumbering, followed by the wheat boom at the turn of the century, and most recently by the spectacular growth of the mineral industries. Each of these was a "leading sector" in the dynamic process whereby their expansion was transmitted to the rest of the economy by means of inter-industry effects, or, in more current terminology, by the setting up of forward and/or backward linkages. This therefore generated the growth in total product which we are now examining.

Most quantitative analyses of this process have been concerned with the demand side of the theory, with little consideration of how the economy was suited to meet these demands. We therefore have very little knowledge of the role played by natural resources as factors of production, either within the staple theory, or for the economy as a whole. Since it is precisely our purpose to evaluate the contribution of resources as inputs into the economic process—specifically the production of goods and services—this analytical gap is rather disconcerting.

One of the most important natural resources is land. However, theory is far from clear on how to evaluate its role. Ricardian treatment considers land to be a passive element in production, for rent is seen to arise as a result of differentials in fertility or in location, wherein shifts in the demand curve for a product permit poorer lands to be brought into use, thus generating a surplus on the more advantageous ones. Our contention is that in certain endeavours, particularly primary industries, natural resources enter directly into the production of goods and services in co-operation with labour and reproducible capital. For land, this corresponds to the "original and indestructible power of the soil," mentioned also by Ricardo, but which is not as famous as his more elaborate theory.

While this latter is useful for many areas of economic activity, in particular those where location determines the selection of sites, such as trade, services, transportation, and most manufacturing, it is felt that it does not fully describe the nature of economic production in agriculture, forestry, mining, and hydro-electric power generation. In these sectors, such natural resources as mineral deposits, water resourses, and the classical resource, land, enter as inputs in the production function, as do the other factors of production. As a result their contribution should be evaluated in any attempt to examine the basis of Canada's growth.

The task of deriving these empirical coefficients is made more difficult by a statistical problem. This arises because historically this "bounty of nature" has been regarded as a free good, and no factor payment was made for its use. While no accurate estimates can therefore be made, it is worth seeing how they might be obtained. For several components, we have information on the physical increase in the natural resource.[15] These partial data are presented in Table 9. The mining sector would require a similar type of indicator, such as estimated reserves of mineral wealth. Unfortunately, these data are not readily available.

To use these physical increase series, we require, in addition, a system of weights equal to the share of their earnings in national income. As we have noted, no income is imputed to them, and where some rent does arise, it is intermingled with rent resulting from differentials so that no pure reward for productivity is obtainable. Nonetheless, it is clear that work is badly needed in this area if the elements critical for Canada's economic growth are to be seen in accurate historical perspective.[16]

TABLE 9
GROWTH OF SELECTED NATURAL RESOURCES, CANADA
(percentages)

Indicator of resource growth	Growth rate, 1926-56
Agriculture: area of occupied farms	0.45
Forestry: area of productive forest lands	2.16
Hydro-electric power: energy content of available water power	1.46

SOURCES: DBS, *Canada Year Book*, Agriculture, *1961*, 1250; Forestry, *1926*, 18 and *1957-8*, 39; Hydro, *1926*, 362 and *1957-8*, 559.

IV. TOTAL FACTOR INPUT

Our final task in this chapter is to obtain a weighting scheme whereby we may combine our individual input series into an index of total factor input. As described in the first chapter, this weighting scheme is obtained from the share of the various factors of production in national income. Thus the share of labour is taken as the sum of wages, salaries, and supplementary labour income, together with that part of the net income of individual entrepreneurs that can be allocated to labour. This latter item is not available separately, and it is therefore necessary to estimate it. This is not a simple procedure, for it has been found that if the compensation for labour effort by these entrepreneurs is assumed to be at the same rates as for other workers, the return to capital, obtained as a residual, is unrealistically low. If, on the other hand, we assume that their capital receives a rate of return equivalent to that elsewhere, the return to labour which is now obtained as a residual is apparently too low.[17] To overcome these unsatisfactory results, we neglect the rates of compensation, and take the share of labour and capital in the income of the owners of unincorporated enterprises to be the same as in corporations.[18]

With labour's share thus separated, we further deduct from national income the income received by Canadians from abroad and add back the domestic income paid to foreigners, leaving us with the share of domestic property in national income. This is then subdivided into the returns to the various types of property, such as land, inventories, machinery and equipment, and construction-type capital, in a two-stage process. We first divide total property income into residential rents, property income in the agricultural sector, and residual property income. Then, for each of these classes we subdivide its property income into the four aforementioned types (land, inventories, machinery and equipment, and construction) on the basis of asset structure. This implicitly assumes a similar rate of return to these various types of property within each class.

The theoretical framework for obtaining the factor coefficients is consequently fairly uncomplicated. However, although the share of labour over the entire period may be readily calculated, the refinements required for the property share are available only for the year 1949 for which the inter-industry study was undertaken,[19] and for which there are available data on the magnitude of the various assets,[20] especially land. We are faced therefore with two alternatives: to continue with our detailed analysis, restricted to the coefficients of this single base year, or to consider fewer factors of production and derive the coefficients from the experience of the entire period 1926-56. We have decided to present the results using both of these methods. For the former, we give in Table 10A the allocation of domestic property income, followed by the distribution of national income in 1949 by the factor shares in Table 10B.

TABLE 10A

SHARE OF ASSETS IN DOMESTIC PROPERTY INCOME, CANADA, 1949
(percentages)

Sector	Share in domestic property income	
Agriculture	8.08	
Land		3.74 pp
Construction (excl. residences)		0.79
Machinery & equipment		1.15
Inventories		2.41
Residential	6.32	
Land		0.62
Construction (incl. farm residences)		5.70
Remainder	85.60	
Land		19.94
Construction (incl. gov't. bldg.)		40.84
Machinery & equipment		14.71
Inventories		10.11

The second alternative, wherein the factor coefficients are derived from the share of the various factors in national income over the entire period 1926-56, gives the results as shown in Table 11.

TABLE 10B

DISTRIBUTION OF NATIONAL INCOME BY FACTOR SHARES, CANADA, 1949
(percentages)

Factor of production	Share in national income
Labour °	78.70
Land	5.76
Residential construction	1.35
Other construction	9.87
Machinery and equipment	3.76
Inventories	2.97
Domestic earnings on foreign assets	0.65
Less: Foreign earnings on Canadian assets	− 3.05

  ° Excludes military.
SOURCE: Appendix A-III.

TABLE 11

DISTRIBUTION OF NATIONAL INCOME BY FACTOR SHARES, CANADA, 1926-56
(percentages)

Factor of production	Share in national income
Labour	77.52
Reproducible capital	25.41
Domestic earnings on foreign assets	0.89
Less: Foreign earnings on Canadian assets	− 3.82

The shares of labour and capital are very similar under the two measures. However, in the second case, the fact that the types of capital are not separable means that an oversimplified aggregate is being used. With these factor co-efficients, it is possible to calculate the factor contributions to the growth rate of output. In Table 12, the results of these calculations using the two bases, 1949 and 1926–56, are presented. We consider also the effect of using gross as opposed to net stock measures with the two bases.

In both part A and B of Table 12 we find that the gross stock estimates over-state the capital contribution, but by a rather small amount. Coupled with the smaller capital coefficient relative to labour, this means that the total factor con-tribution—and therefore the residual as well—is only slightly different in the two cases. In addition, we see that the discrepancy arising from the use of the 1949 base, rather than that for the entire period, is negligible.

Three significant results emerge from these findings. The first is that despite its relatively small coefficient, the growth of capital has been so great in this period as to make it almost as significant a factor of production as labour, adjusted for changes in quality. In addition, the role of the residual has been striking, accounting for no less than seventy per cent of the growth rate. Finally, we see that the role of foreigners has been very small, amounting to less than two per cent of the growth rate. This is not to deprecate the role of the foreigner in Canadian economic growth, for associated with foreign enterprise is a host of induced domestic activities. In subsequent chapters we shall return to this matter,[21] and simply wish at present to provide some perspective for evaluating the direct impact of this factor.

TABLE 12A

FACTOR CONTRIBUTIONS TO THE GROWTH RATE, CANADA, 1949 BASE

(percentages)

Input	Contribution to the growth rate [*]					
	Gross stock			Net stock		
Labour			0.66			0.66
Man-hours		0.57			0.57	
Labour force	1.20			1.20		
Average annual hours	−0.63			−0.63		
Quality change		0.09			0.09	
Education	0.17			0.17		
Age-sex composition	−0.09			−0.09		
Domestic property			0.55			0.52
Land (agriculture only)		0.03			0.03	
Residential construction		0.04			0.03	
Other construction		0.25			0.20	
Machinery and equipment		0.17			0.20	
Inventories		0.06			0.06	
Foreign capital owned by Canadians			0.02			0.02
Less: Capital in Canada owned						
by foreigners			−0.05			−0.05
Total factor input			1.18			1.15
Residual contribution			2.71			2.74
Growth rate			3.89			3.89

[*] The figures are all percentage points.

TABLE 12B

FACTOR CONTRIBUTIONS TO THE GROWTH RATE, CANADA, 1926-56 BASE

(percentages)

Input	Contribution to growth rate	
	Gross stock	Net stock
Labour	0.65	0.65
Domestic capital [*]	0.64	0.56
Foreign capital owned by Canadians	0.03	0.03
Less: Capital in Canada owned		
by foreigners	−0.06	−0.06
Total factor input	1.26	1.18
Residual contribution	2.63	2.71

[*] Excludes land.

To conclude this chapter, we shall compare these results for Canada with Denison's findings for the United States.[22] The latter has been revised with respect to the labour component to conform to our concepts.[23] Since he uses gross stock figures, we shall use our corresponding figures to ensure comparability. The United States estimates are summarized in Table 13.

Denison's own treatment of labour suggests that its contribution was about twice as much—1.57 percentage points of the growth rate—making the total factor contribution 2.00 percentage points, and leaving a residual of 0.93 per cent. The differences are substantial and our reasons for rejecting several of his refinements have already been discussed.

TABLE 13

FACTOR CONTRIBUTIONS TO THE GROWTH RATE, US, 1929-57 BASE
(percentages)

Input		Contribution to the growth rate
Labour		0.82
Man-hours		0.47
Labour force	1.00	
Average annual hours	−0.53	
Quality change		0.36
Education	0.35	
Age-sex composition	0.01	
Domestic Capital		0.41
Non-farm residential construction		0.05
Other construction and machinery		
and equipment		0.28
Land		0.00
Inventories		0.08
Foreign capital owned by Americans		0.02
Less: Capital in US owned by foreigners		0.00
Total factor input		1.25
Residual contribution		1.68
Growth rate		2.93

Comparing his modified results with ours yields several interesting observations. The most obvious is that, despite the much more significant role played by capital in Canada's growth, it has not been so great as to offset the lower relative contribution of labour as compared to the United States,[24] with the result that total factor input has increased slightly faster in the United States. Since Canada's growth rate has been noted to be higher than of the United States,[25] we conclude that the residual must have been a more important element in Canada. This is in fact what we observe in Tables 12 and 13, where the residual accounts for over 70 per cent of the growth rate of GNP in Canada as compared to slightly over one-half in the United States.

Thus it is necessary to focus attention on the nature of the residual on two accounts; because of its absolute size which makes it the single most important factor in recent economic growth in both countries, and because of the greater importance of the residual in Canada, both absolutely and relative to the growth rate. This examination will be undertaken by departing from the hitherto highly aggregative analysis and considering instead the various sectors of the economy. In this way, the loci wherein productivity advance has been most important can be determined, and the factors underlying the results may be searched for.

CHAPTER FOUR

CONTRIBUTION OF INTER-INDUSTRY SHIFTS, CANADA, 1937-61

IN THIS CHAPTER, the performance of the major sectors within the Canadian economy is investigated. The model used earlier to analyse aggregate behaviour is used also here to discover how labour, capital, and technological change have contributed to the growth of output in each industry, and to relate the behaviour of the individual industries to the performance of the total economy.

One problem that immediately presents itself is the use of constant returns to scale at this level of dis-aggregation. It has been suggested that in advanced societies resource industries tend to operate under decreasing returns and that perhaps other sectors undergo increasing returns.[1] Unfortunately, there is little empirical evidence regarding these phenomena. Rather than insert an arbitrary estimate, we shall for the present retain the assumption of constant returns. When sufficient evidence has been gathered to indicate that the sum of the factor coefficients should total more or less than one, the results can be modified accordingly.

Several changes in our basic framework must be made at this point. Because of the lack of deflated output series by industry prior to 1935, it is necessary to shorten the period to be studied. The calculation of such series is more complicated than that of the aggregate output estimates. The latter takes deflated GNE as a proxy for real GNP, whereas at the industry level, it is necessary to take into consideration the problem of double counting. The present treatment is to deflate the value added by each industry.[2] As these data do not go back as far as 1926, and since there are no other estimates of comparable quality to which they could be linked, it has been necessary to change the terminal years. Thus, 1937 and 1961 have been chosen as the best possible compromise between a sufficiently long period and the choice of years in similar cyclical conditions.[3] These are not years of full capacity utilization, so that the growth rate over this period cannot be viewed as potential economic growth, as could that for the years 1926 to 1956.

One final comment on these new output data is necessary. They are given on a gross domestic product (GDP) basis, thereby differing from the GNP figures by international income flows and by indirect taxes and subsidies which convert the factor cost data of GDP to market prices for GNP. The effect of this transformation on the growth rate in the period 1937–61 is to reduce it from 4.62 per cent (GNP) to 4.57 per cent (GDP). The lower rate of growth of the latter is the result of the growth of indirect taxes and subsidies as well as international income payments, which surpassed the growth of GNP over this period.[4]

Table 14 presents the growth rates for the major industrial groupings and for the total GDP. In addition, the growth of labour input fully adjusted for quality change is presented.

There appears to be some association between the rate of growth of output and

TABLE 14

GROWTH OF OUTPUT AND LABOUR BY INDUSTRY, CANADA, 1937-61
(percentages)

Industry	Average annual rate of growth	
	Output	Adjusted labour
Agriculture	1.18	− 1.77
Forestry, fishing, trapping	1.75	− 1.07
Mining, quarrying, oil wells	5.44	0.51
Manufacturing	5.22	2.25
Construction	5.68	3.30
Electric power and gas utilities	8.36	3.72
Trade, wholesale, and retail	4.72	2.97
Finance, insurance and real estate	4.54	3.64
Transportation, storage, and communication	5.31	1.83
Commercial and community services	3.85	3.82
Total, ten industries *	4.54	0.82

* We have excluded from our estimates public administration, defence, and the "other goods-producing" industries. Output for these grew at 5.44 and 3.24 per cent, the net effect being to raise the growth rate of GDP to 4.57 per cent.

SOURCES: Output, text preceding this table; Labour, Table B-17.

that of labour input, particularly at the extremes. Thus, agriculture and forestry, with output growing more slowly than the aggregate, show a decline in labour input, while electric power and gas utilities and construction, with very high rates of output growth, had high growth rates of labour input as well. The clear association here is dimmed in the intermediate ranges, however, by such industries as mining, with high growth rates of output and low rates for labour, and services, with a relatively low output growth rate but a high rate of growth of labour. Much of this is due to the role of capital in the production functions, and it is therefore necessary to derive estimates for this latter factor of production.

Once again we are faced with an absence of sufficiently long capital stock estimates and are compelled to prepare our own. The details are too numerous to be included in the text and we have consequently placed them together with sources and methods in Appendix B-I. The growth rates, for both net and gross stock, obtained from these estimates are presented in Table 15. The inability to obtain good constant dollar inventory estimates, together with the relatively small weight of this component of capital led us to omit it from the capital figures.[5] In addition, the conversion to a domestic product concept for measuring output has obviated the need to allocate part of the growth of output to foreigners.

It is difficult to discover a significant degree of association between the rates of growth of capital and of output. This puts the notion of a constant capital-output ratio at the industry level into doubt. Since this ratio has such a prominent place in the literature of economic growth, it is instructive to examine its course over time for these ten industries (Table 16).

Despite the rise of the capital-output ratio in agriculture, forestry, fishing and trapping, mining, and construction, its decline in the remaining sectors has been so great that the aggregate ratio has been reduced by almost one-quarter, using both the gross and the net measures. Thus, any assumption of stability in this ratio for the Canadian economy is unwarranted. The use of a constant capital

TABLE 15

GROWTH RATES OF CAPITAL BY INDUSTRY, CANADA, 1937-61
(percentages)

Industry	Net stock		Gross stock	
	Construction	Machinery and Equipment	Construction	Machinery and Equipment
Agriculture	3.32	5.19	1.47	5.07
Forestry, fishing, trapping	5.89	4.41	5.51	4.50
Mining, quarrying, oil wells	7.66	6.37	6.90	6.05
Manufacturing	2.28	4.59	1.54	3.76
Construction	4.09	8.73	2.62	7.25
Electric power and gas utilities	5.91	5.99	5.81	5.10
Trade, wholesale and retail	3.31	8.02	3.07	7.29
Finance, insurance, real estate	3.50	8.18	3.20	6.77
Transportation, storage, communication	1.08	5.82	0.93	5.34
Commercial and community services	2.90	7.58	2.60	6.52

SOURCES: Tables B-1 through B-11, A-1.

TABLE 16

CAPITAL-OUTPUT RATIOS, CANADA, 1937 AND 1961

Industry	Net stock/NDP		Gross stock/GDP	
	1937	1961	1937	1961
Agriculture	0.78	1.86	1.57	2.83
Forestry, fishing, trapping	0.29	0.71	0.51	1.10
Mining, quarrying, oil wells	0.87	1.39	1.35	1.77
Manufacturing	2.27	1.41	3.85	2.13
Construction	0.22	0.33	0.51	0.55
Electric power and gas utilities	19.31	8.20	16.73	9.05
Trade, wholesale and retail	0.98	0.91	1.53	1.35
Finance, insurance, real estate	16.96	11.78	19.42	13.28
Transportation, storage, communication	12.39	4.76	14.38	6.55
Commercial and community services	2.62	2.36	4.19	3.48
Aggregate	3.20	2.62	5.02	3.68

SOURCES: Capital, Tables B-1 through B-11; Output, DBS, Occasional Paper 61-505, *Indexes of Real Domestic Product by Industry of Origin, 1935-61* (Ottawa, 1963), and DBS 61-005, *Annual Supplement to the Monthly Index of Industrial Production* (Ottawa, 1966).

output ratio requires a theory indicating how the ratios in the various industries interact to generate the aggregate constant ratio. Neglect of this step has no doubt led to a too casual use of this ratio.

With the estimates of the growth rates of the factors of production now available for the period 1937–61, it is possible to evaluate the contribution of these factors to the growth of output in each of these industries. A set of coefficients is required for this purpose, and the inter-industry table for 1949 provides us with the necessary detail.[6] Once more the labour share is taken as the sum of wages and salaries and supplementary labour income, plus the proportion of net income going to individual entrepreneurs that is allocable to labour effort. The share going to property is divided among construction and machinery and equipment on the basis of their respective shares in net stock in 1949 (Table 17).

TABLE 17
FACTOR COEFFICIENTS BY INDUSTRY, CANADA, 1949

Industry	Labour	Capital	Machinery and Equipment	Construction
Agriculture	0.788	0.212	0.146	0.066
Forestry, fishing, trapping	0.785	0.215	0.123	0.092
Mining, quarrying, oil wells	0.590	0.410	0.137	0.273
Manufacturing	0.737	0.263	0.135	0.128
Construction	0.941	0.059	0.046	0.013
Electric power and gas utilities	0.399	0.601	0.139	0.462
Trade, wholesale and retail	0.773	0.227	0.055	0.172
Finance, insurance, real estate	0.412	0.588	—	0.588
Transportation, storage, communication	0.773	0.227	0.070	0.157
Commercial and community services	0.898	0.102	0.013	0.089

It is instructive to compare the value of these coefficients of the various industries with those for roughly similar industries in the Norwegian economy. These are derived from Johansen's study. For three sectors—agriculture, mining, and electric power—he assumes scale coefficients of less than one, as can be seen from Table 18.

TABLE 18
FACTOR COEFFICIENTS IN THE NORWEGIAN ECONOMY

Industry	Labour	Capital	Scale coefficient
Agriculture	0.46	0.20	0.66
Forestry	0.64	0.36	1.0
Mining	0.52	0.38	0.90
Construction	0.88	0.12	1.0
Electric power	0.30	0.60	0.90
Trade	0.53	0.47	1.0
Dwellings	0.03	0.97	1.0
Services	0.86	0.14	1.0

SOURCE: Johansen, *A Multi-sectoral Study of Economic Growth*, 74, Table 5.2, 4.

Lacking any basis for adjusting our own scale coefficients we have decided to leave them at one. Thus, our estimates for the agriculture, mining, and electric power sectors are not directly comparable with Johansen's. Nevertheless, there is a great deal of similarity in the orders of magnitude of these coefficients for like industries. This suggests that the general characteristics of the various industries have much in common in the two countries, although there is a tendency for industries in Canada to have a slightly higher labour coefficient. This stems mostly from the way in which we have estimated the labour component in the income of individual entrepreneurs.

Weighting the growth rates of labour and capital by these coefficients gives us the contribution of these factors to the growth of output on an industrial basis.

These results are presented in Table 19.

TABLE 19

FACTOR CONTRIBUTIONS TO THE GROWTH RATE, CANADA, 1937-61
(percentages)

Industry	Growth rate output	Labour contri- bution	Capital contri- bution	Total factor contri- bution	Residual contri- bution
Agriculture	1.18	− 1.40	0.98	− 0.42	1.60
Forestry, fishing, trapping	1.75	− 0.84	1.08	0.24	1.51
Mining, quarrying, oil wells	5.44	0.30	2.96	3.26	2.18
Manufacturing	5.22	1.66	0.91	2.57	2.65
Construction	5.68	3.10	0.46	3.56	2.12
Electric power and gas utilities	8.36	1.48	3.56	5.05	3.31
Trade, wholesale and retail	4.72	2.30	1.01	3.31	1.41
Finance, insurance, real estate	4.54	1.50	2.08	3.58	0.96
Transportation, storage, communication	5.31	1.42	0.58	1.99	3.32
Commercial and community services	3.85	3.43	0.36	3.79	0.06
	(1)	(2)	(3)	(4)	(5)

SOURCES: (1), Table 14; (2), Labour of Table 17 times (6) Table B-17; (3), Capital, Table 17 times net stock, Table 15; (4), (2) plus (3); (5), (1) minus (4).

Table 19 is a summary of a great deal of data, and the findings must be con-sidered with care. For instance, one is tempted to conclude that there is strong association between the growth of the residual and the growth of output. How-ever, because the residual is a component of the latter, the problem of identifi-cation is encountered. A more meaningful basis for discovering such an associa-tion is the share of the various components in the growth rate. Table 20 divides the above contributions into shares for such a comparison.

TABLE 20

FACTOR SHARES IN THE GROWTH RATE OF OUTPUT, CANADA, 1937-61
(percentages)

Industry	Labour	Capital	Residual
Agriculture	− 118.22	82.80	135.42
Forestry, fishing, trapping	− 48.00	61.94	86.06
Mining, quarrying, oil wells	5.51	54.41	40.07
Manufacturing	31.80	17.43	50.77
Construction	54.67	8.01	37.32
Electric power and gas utilities	17.70	42.58	39.59
Trade, wholesale and retail	48.64	21.40	29.96
Finance, insurance, real estate	33.04	50.68	16.28
Transportation, storage, communication	26.65	10.87	62.49
Commercial and community services	89.09	9.27	1.64

This table reveals that no simple association exists between the residual con-tribution and the growth rate of output. In fact, the sectors with the greatest relative residual contribution—agriculture and forestry—have the lowest growth rates of output. Capital has had a predominant role in these same two industries, as well as in mining, electric power, finance, insurance, and real estate (because of the residential construction component in this sector). Only in construction, trade, and services has labour been the greatest contributor to the growth of output. It appears from this analysis that any attempt to isolate one factor as the key to growth in all sectors of the economy would grossly distort the true situation.

Our analysis for the period 1926-56, in which we considered only aggregates, indicated that the most important element was the residual which we found contributed more than 70 per cent of the growth rate. To make the aggregate measure comparable with the findings in Table 19, it is necessary to make some minor alterations. The period covered is now 1937-61, and the output is measured on a domestic basis. Also, the lack of industrial data on inventories and on international income flows means that we must use a narrower concept of capital including only such reproducible capital as machinery and equipment and construction-type. Finally, as we have excluded government from our industrial distribution, it is necessary to remove it from the aggregates as well. The growth rates of these revised aggregates are presented in Table 21A and the contribution of aggregate labour and capital to the growth rate of output for both the 1937-61 period and the 1926-56 period are given in Table 21B.

TABLE 21A

AVERAGE ANNUAL RATES OF GROWTH,
CANADA, 1937-61
(percentages)

Aggregate output	4.54
Aggregate Capital	
Machinery and equipment	5.08
Construction	3.20
Aggregate labour	0.83

SOURCES: Output, Table 14; Capital, Tables B-1 to B-11; Labour, Table B-17 (6).

TABLE 21B

FACTOR CONTRIBUTIONS TO THE GROWTH RATE, CANADA, 1937-61
(percentages)

		1937-61	1926-56
Aggregate capital		0.82	0.50
machinery and equipment	0.40		
construction	0.43		
Aggregate labour		0.65	0.66
Aggregate residual		3.07	2.73
Growth rate		4.54	3.89

SOURCES: 1926-56, Table 12A, net stock variant; 1937-61, weighted Labour with 0.789, Machinery and equipment with 0.078 and Construction, 0.133. From DBS, *Inter-industry Flow*, Table 1.

The labour and residual components are not very different in the shorter period, and the bulk of the discrepancy in the growth rate is due to the much greater capital contribution during the years 1937-61. As a result, our earlier findings for the contribution of the aggregates to the growth of output apply reasonably well to this more limited period. In particular, the residual is about the same proportion of the growth rate as it was between 1926 and 1956—68 versus 70 per cent.

This latter preponderance of the residual does not appear in Table 20, where only agriculture, forestry, transportation, storage, and communication contain residuals that account for more than two-thirds of their growth rates, which is approximately the share of the aggregate residual in the aggregate rate of growth. Furthermore, the rate of growth of the aggregate residual of Table 21B is higher than that of the various industries with the exception of electric power and gas utilities, transportation, storage, and communication, as given in Table 19 (5). Since the former is a weighted average of the industries' residuals, there appears to be a serious inconsistency between our findings for the aggregate economy and those for its underlying components.

Some process is occuring in the economy which our aggregate measures do not sense, and which may conceivably be leading to an overstatement of the role played by the aggregate residual. Because our detailed study for the years 1926-56 was a highly aggregative one, it is crucial that an explanation of these conflicting results be found. The study of the industrial components and their relationship to the aggregate will provide us with what is perhaps the key factor in the observed disparity. This may be referred to as the "inter-industry shift" in the structure of production. An often-used indicator of this process is the share of output produced in each of the industries at the beginning and at the end of the period. Such a measure is given for the years 1937 and 1961 in Table 22, where the shares are in current dollars of output.

TABLE 22

INDUSTRIAL DISTRIBUTION OF GROSS OUTPUT, CANADA, 1937 AND 1961
(percentages)

Industry	Share in GDP (current prices)	
	1937	1961
Agriculture	10.3	4.6
Forestry, fishing, trapping	2.2	1.4
Mining, quarrying, oil wells	7.0	4.3
Manufacturing	24.9	25.9
Construction	3.3	5.5
Electric power and gas utilities	2.0	3.4
Trade, wholesale and retail	12.9	14.1
Finance, insurance, real estate	9.8	10.6
Transportation, storage, communication	10.6	9.1
Commercial and community services	12.2	13.4
Public administration and defence	4.8	7.7

SOURCE: DBS, *National Accounts, 1926-56,* 28; *1961,* 16.

While Table 22 is useful to illustrate the changes that have occurred in the relative importance of different industries, we require a rather more sophisticated set of analytical tools if we are to evaluate the net effect of this phenomenon upon our measures of growth. Our procedure will be to calculate the impact of the changing relative importance of each of the industries in the over-all growth process.

The first step is to reconsider the meaningfulness of our factor measures. We have thus far standardized labour input for several of the main causes of differences in its quality—namely, education, hours, and age and sex. Thus it could be assumed that labour in each industry was of homogeneous quality. In our aggregative analysis, we once more standardized the labour component for these items. But in this instance, there is a further implicit assumption that labour in different industries, once it has been adjusted for the quality differences, is a homogeneous input. It is this assumption that is now being questioned. If we take the amount of national income going to labour in each industry in the base year (1949), and divide this by standardized labour input in the respective industries in the same year, we obtain an estimate of the compensation of a unit of standardized labour input in each industry in 1949. Taking the property income in each industry and dividing it by the base year net stock gives the implicit rate of return to property. The results of these procedures are presented in Table 23.

TABLE 23
IMPLICIT FACTOR PAYMENTS BY INDUSTRY, CANADA, 1949

Industry	Income per standard labor input [*]	Rate of return to property
	$	%
Agriculture	0.47	15.32
Forestry, fishing, trapping	0.86	36.78
Mining, quarrying, oil wells	1.84	43.91
Manufacturing	1.38	19.13
Construction	1.73	22.87
Electric power and gas utilities	1.05	6.21
Trade, wholesale and retail	1.29	30.60
Finance, insurance, real estate	1.53	4.53
Transportation, storage, communication	1.28	5.40
Commercial and community services	0.80	6.07
Aggregate	1.04	10.09

[*] Per man-hour adjusted for education, age, and sex.
SOURCES: Table B-14 (4) and (5).

Our estimates of average income per standardized unit of labour input show approximately the variation we would expect. However, the wide variation in the return to property requires some explanation. It is due mainly to our deficient estimates of real property to which we allocate the entire non-labour share of national income. It will be remembered that we have been able to estimate only reproducible capital by industry—that is, machinery and equipment, and construction—omitting inventories and land, as well as natural resources. If the latter were to be included in mining and forestry, the unrealistically high returns of Table 23 would be greatly reduced. No doubt the inclusion of inventories in trade and land in agriculture would similarly reduce the high returns in those sectors.

As we shall indicate later, this problem does not affect our analysis. None-theless, wide variations in the true return to property would still occur, much as in the labour returns. This is due to a number of structural and institutional peculiarities of the different industries. Among structural factors one must con-sider the availability of complementary factors in the production process, the nature of the entrepreneurial function, the supply elasticities of factors of produc-tion, and so forth. Institutional elements, such as collective-bargaining proce-dures, market structure, and legal provisions for the internalizing of economies through patents and royalties enter to create differentials in the average compen-sation of otherwise similar factors of production.

As an example, we may consider the relatively low return to capital in the electric power and gas utilities. This is the result of the decision-making process. in that industry. With much of it owned by provincial governments, and with regulation by public bodies in a good part of the remainder, investment plans are made in the light of social benefit-social cost considerations rather than on the basis of the profit maximizing calculus inherent in the purely competitive situation.

These sources of variation in the effectiveness of the various factors of produc-tion clearly indicate that it is too gross a simplification to treat factors in different industries as essentially homogeneous. Since our estimates of factor contributions in the aggregative data do precisely that, it is necessary to revise them. This is done by evaluating the change in output that has resulted from factors shifting to different industries without any increase in their numbers. This term had originally been included in the aggregate residual, and we are obliged to remove this shift component from the residual and to combine it with the contribution resulting from the growth of factor inputs to get a more accurate estimate of total factor contribution.

The extent of these inter-industry shifts can be measured in two ways: the first assumes what we shall call a relationship of strict complementarity between labour and capital in the production functions of all industries, while the second assumes one of substitution. By the former, we mean that when labour moves from industry "A" to industry "B" it is provided with the same complex of inputs that other units of labour in "B"possess, so that its marginal productivity becomes the same as that of labour in "B". The change in the production functions of both "A" and "B" is solely one of scale as the proportions are taken as fixed. The second assumption reduces all inputs to a common denominator. Whenever a unit of input shifts to another industry, its average product becomes the same as that of each unit of input in the new industry.

Measurement of inter-industry shifts under these assumptions is based on the condition discussed earlier that the compensation of factors reflects their marginal productivity. Weighing the share of the various industries in standardized labour input in 1937 and in 1961 by the average compensation of a unit of such labour in 1949 in each industry gives an estimate of the change in output per unit of labour that would result from redistributing the labour force only and its provision with complementary factors in the new industry to which it has shifted.

The calculations made following this procedure indicate that the shift of labour would have raised its per unit output by 20.39 per cent over the period. We do not calculate the effect of shifts in the shares of capital because of the partial coverage of our capital data, to which we have previously referred. Before entering into a discussion of this result, we proceed to derive the alternative estimate, based on the assumption of substitution (Table 24).

TABLE 24

INDUSTRY SHARES IN STANDARD LABOUR INPUT, CANADA, 1937 AND 1961

Industry	Labour compensation	Shares in labour	
	1949	1937	1961
	(dollars)	(percentages)	(percentages)
Agriculture	0.47	41.40	14.86
Forestry, fishing, trapping	0.86	4.24	2.34
Mining, quarrying, oil wells	1.84	2.41	2.12
Manufacturing	1.38	16.99	22.26
Construction	1.73	4.12	7.00
Electric power and gas utilities	1.05	0.60	1.11
Trade, wholesale and retail	1.29	9.88	15.66
Finance, insurance, real estate	1.53	1.89	3.47
Transportation, storage, communication	1.28	5.94	7.15
Commercial and community services	0.80	12.53	27.04

SOURCES: Tables B-14 and B-15.

The weighting scheme for this part of the analysis of inter-industry shifts is the average return to a standardized unit of labour input. The combination of factors into an index of total input is complicated by the heterogeneity of the components. Our procedure has been to measure all inputs in terms of labour equivalents because we have already standardized the labour factor for differences in physically discernible attributes, such as hours worked, education, and age and sex. The reduction to labour equivalents was accomplished by assigning to each unit of standardized labour input a weight of unity and then assigning to each unit of capital a weight equal to the ratio of its marginal productivity to that of a unit of labour in the same industry. Thus, the marginal rate of substitution between labour and capital is taken as fixed within each industry. This procedure has the added advantage of offsetting the omission of other than reproducible capital, which was discussed in our evaluation of Table 23, by assigning a higher weight to the volume of reproducible capital.

An example will make this calculation clear. In agriculture, one standard man-hour of work received forty-seven cents. Reproducible capital in that sector earned a rate of return of about 15 per cent. (See Table 23). Thus, one dollar of reproducible capital in that industry is as productive as 0.15/0.47 man-hours of labour. To the extent that this rate of return is too high because of the exclusion of land's contribution, the exclusion is fully compensated for by attributing to reproducible capital an inflated weight. Deriving weights for the conversion of capital into labour equivalents in other industries in a similar manner permits us to estimate total factor input in labour equivalents in any year.[7] With labour standardized, these combined inputs are also comparable between industries enabling us to estimate the share of the various industries in total factor input in 1937 and in 1961. Weighting these shares by the average return to a unit of standardized labour input in the different industries, presented in Table 23, gives the effect of shifts of productive factors between industries on the growth of output per unit of combined factor input. Table 25 gives the share of the industries in total input. The weighted sums show that output per unit of combined input would have increased by 17.3 per cent because of the shifts of factors between industries. In terms of an annual rate of growth, this amounts to 0.66 per cent.

TABLE 25

DISTRIBUTION OF TOTAL FACTOR INPUT BY INDUSTRY, CANADA,
1937 AND 1961
(percentages)

Industry	Share in total inputs measured in labour equivalents	
	1937	1961
Agriculture	36.82	16.22
Forestry, fishing, trapping	3.82	2.49
Mining, quarrying, oil wells	3.01	5.14
Manufacturing	18.34	21.51
Construction	3.46	5.15
Electric power and gas utilities	1.37	3.02
Trade, wholesale and retail	10.50	15.01
Finance, insurance, real estate	3.95	5.91
Transportation, storage, communication	6.86	6.99
Commercial and community services	11.87	18.55

SOURCE: Table B-16.

This latter method, based on substitutional relationships, is preferred because it avoids the problem of double counting that is encountered when we assume complementarity. This double counting arises because we have maintained that when labour moves between industries, capital as well as other factors shift to maintain constant factor proportions in each industry. But if labour moved from a less to a more capital-intensive industry, an increase in the total supply of capital would be required if factor proportions are to remain unchanged in the new industry. Since our earlier analysis has already accounted for increases in factor supplies, the contribution of this accommodating increase in capital will be counted twice, explaining the lower increase in output from inter-industry shifts under the substitution case. We shall use the latter results in the remainder of this section.

The findings enable us to explain the fact that the residual contribution for the aggregated data is so much greater than that for most of the individual industries. The discrepancy arises because the former considers all labour in the economy, adjusted for physical quality differences, to be equally productive, and similarly all capital. Thus, the total labour input is considered to increase by the same factor as the growth in standardized man-hours. It has been our contention that factors are not at all equally productive in different industries for many reasons. One such reason, which we may soon be able to quantify, is the difference in on-the-job training between industries. Others, such as attitude to risk, market structure, entrepreneurial skill, and the like, present very serious measurement problems. We have combined these effects and have maintained that differences in factor productivity are due to these institutional characteristics. Hence, the shift of labour and capital into industries with different characteristics will no doubt alter their productivity and thereby directly affect the level of output. We propose to attribute the growth of output resulting from these shifts to the factors themselves, removing this component from the otherwise overstated residual (Table 26).

TABLE 26
Sources of Growth, Canada, 1937-61
(percentages)

Average annual rate of growth		4.54	
Direct factor inputs: labour	0.65		
capital	0.82		
Indirect factor inputs	0.66		1.47
Total factor inputs		2.13	
Residual contribution		2.41	

It is not possible to precisely substantiate the findings from the industrial data because of the nature of the functions we have used. [8] An approximation can be made, however, in the following manner. Evaluate the contribution of each industry to the growth of aggregate output by weighting its own growth rate of output by the share of that industry in total output in the base year (1949). The next step is to estimate the industrial contribution to the growth of total input by weighting their respective growth rates of total factor input by the base year share of that industry in total factor input. Subtracting its input contribution from its output contribution gives an estimate of that industry's contribution to the growth of the aggregate residual. The results of this test are given in Table 27.

TABLE 27
Industrial Contributions to the Growth Rate, Canada, 1937-61
(percentages)

Industry	Contribution to growth of total output	Contribution to growth of total input	Contribution to residual
Agriculture	0.13	−0.10	0.24
Forestry, fishing, trapping	0.05	0.01	0.04
Mining, quarrying, oil wells	0.19	0.08	0.10
Manufacturing	1.51	0.60	0.91
Construction	0.38	0.18	0.21
Electric power and gas utilities	0.15	0.09	0.06
Trade, wholesale and retail	0.73	0.41	0.32
Finance, insurance, real estate	0.44	0.15	0.29
Transportation, storage, communication	0.47	0.14	0.33
Commercial and community services	0.42	0.57	−0.15
Total contribution	4.47	2.13	2.34

Source: Table B-18.

While these totals do not exactly correspond to the aggregates of Table 26 because of a certain amount of interaction they are sufficiently close to suggest that the allocation of that part of output arising from inter-industry shifts to a separate cause is a necessary step in the reconciliation of the aggregative data with our industrial findings.

The negative sign of the residual contribution of the service industry may at first seem puzzling, but it is readily explained. What we have done is to derive a type of average from the various components. Since the share of services in inputs is so much greater than its share in output, and since both inputs and outputs grew at approximately the same rate, the service sector acted as a drag on the rest of the economy by using a certain share of the inputs to produce a proportionately smaller share of output.

Table 27 serves to reduce a substantial amount of information on Canada's economic growth to manageable proportions. From it one can identify the major contributors to the growth of total product, the most important users of the growing supply of factor inputs, and the main areas of productivity advance. In addition, these roles can be discussed in systematic fashion, because this description of growth is in quantitative terms.

The sector that has contributed most substantially to growth in Canada is manufacturing. Its factor contribution accounted for over one-fourth of the total factor contribution, and its share in the aggregate residual was more than 35 per cent. Thus, growth within manufacturing alone has accounted for about one-third of the growth of aggregate output in Canada.

Trade is next in terms of over-all influence on the growth rate, accounting for about one-sixth of the total. This is a result of a 20 per cent share in total input contribution and a 15 per cent share in the aggregate residual.

It must be observed, however, that many important facets of growth are not covered within such a framework. Perhaps the most important is the lack of any analysis of the commodity flows between industries, such as is provided by input-output models. It is well known that much of the manufacturing industry in Canada is devoted to the processing of primary products, and, as a result, part of the expansion of manufacturing must be explained by the development of the primary industries. In addition, many services have been promoted by the expansion of manufacturing, and they in turn often facilitate the opening of virgin areas for further exploitation of Canada's natural resources. We do not intend to engage in such an analysis, but merely wish to stress the limited scope of our model in the description of economic growth.

One problem in the foregoing study of industrial growth is the unusually low residual in trade, finance, insurance and real estate, and services as can be seen in Table 19. This is the result of the very great difficulties encountered in the measurement of output in these industries. The usual expedient has been to employ an index of inputs, which yields the spurious low residuals which we observe. As a result, we propose to study the performance of those sectors where this problem does not arise, to see whether our conclusions thus far remain valid. The procedures followed are identical to those for the ten sector case. The aggregates, the performance of which is summarized in Table 28, are less inclusive here and this should be kept in mind when comparisons are made with the previous analysis.

This procedure naturally leads to a much greater total residual contribution,

TABLE 28A

GROWTH RATES FOR THE SEVEN-SECTOR
AGGREGATE °, CANADA. 1937-61
(percentages)

Output	4.49
Labour	−0.31
Capital:	
Machinery and equipment	4.71
Construction	2.94

° Includes agriculture, forestry, mining, manufacturing, construction, electric power and gas,
transportation, storage, and communication.

TABLE 28B

SOURCES OF GROWTH FOR THE SEVEN-SECTOR
AGGREGATE
(percentages)

Capital:		0.86
Machinery and equipment	0.39	
Construction	0.47	
Labour		−0.24
Total factor input		0.62
Residual contribution		3.87

since we have removed those industries with low residuals. To evaluate the
impact of inter-industry shifts within this narrower aggregate, the same techniques
are employed as were used for the initial variant. For what we have called the
complementarity case, we use the same weights as earlier for the relevant industries. It is necessary to revise the shares of the various industries in the smaller
"labour force." Table 29 gives the data required for this calculation.

TABLE 29

SEVEN-SECTOR INTER-INDUSTRY SHIFTS, CANADA, 1937-61
COMPLEMENTARITY CASE

Industry	Labour compensation	Shares in labour	
		1937	1961
	$	%	%
Agriculture	0.47	54.69	26.14
Forestry, fishing, trapping	0.86	5.60	4.12
Mining, quarrying, oil wells	1.84	3.18	3.72
Manufacturing	1.38	22.45	39.17
Construction	1.73	5.44	12.31
Electric power and gas utilities	1.05	0.79	1.95
Transportation, storage, communication	1.28	7.85	12.58
	(1)	(2)	(3)

SOURCES: (1), Table B-14 (4); (2) and (3), Table B-15 (1) and (3).

The weighted sums indicate a 32.57 per cent increase in output per man-hour over the period, which is an average annual rate of growth of 1.18 per cent. The effect of implementing the substitution case is derived from weighting the shares given in Table 30 by the earnings per unit of standard labour input.

TABLE 30

SEVEN-SECTION INTER-INDUSTRY SHIFTS, CANADA, 1937-61
SUBSTITUTION CASE
(percentages)

Industry	Share in total input measured in labour equivalents	
	1937	1961
Agriculture	49.27	26.08
Forestry, fishing, trapping	5.10	4.01
Mining, quarrying, oil wells	4.02	8.28
Manufacturing	26.01	37.25
Construction	4.62	8.29
Electric power and gas utilities	1.83	4.86
Transportation, storage, communication	9.16	11.24

SOURCE: Table B-16 (5) and (7).

For this case, the shift of factors between industries would have increased their output by 25.64 per cent, implying an average annual rate of growth of 0.96 per cent. Once again it can be observed that the substitution case gives a slightly lower result because of the problem of double counting. The seven-sector aggregate can therefore be revised to take into account the inter-industry component that has been isolated.

The inter-industry component here is much greater than in the ten-sector variant, mainly because stress is placed on the shift of factors out of agriculture into manufacturing, with no offset being made for the coincident shift into the omitted industries where earnings per unit of standard input are generally lower than in manufacturing. The input of the direct factors is so much less, however, that total factor inputs are much lower in the seven-sector aggregate. The result of these differences is that the intra-industry growth of the residual is much greater in the latter case, as we would expect. These findings can be tested by means of the procedure underlying Table 27. The relevant data are given in Table 32.

Once again this test indicates that the adjustment for inter-industry shifts is necessary, for the totals in Table 31 are very similar to those in Table 32. Most of the discrepancy can be explained by our choice of 1949 as the base year for the test. To the extent that the shares of the various industries in output and in inputs over the entire period are not accurately represented by the 1949 shares, the results are biased. Fortunately, this bias is small, and the findings uphold our contention that inter-industry shifts have been of critical importance in Canada in this period, and must be removed from the residual as a result to avoid serious overstatement of the role of technological progress.

Kendrick places great emphasis on the importance of this adjustment of factor inputs in terms of their relative compensation:

TABLE 31

SOURCES OF GROWTH, SEVEN SECTORS, CANADA, 1937-61
(percentages)

Average annual growth rate of output		4.49
Direct factor inputs: Labour	−0.24	
Capital	0.86	
	0.62	
Indirect factor inputs	0.96	
Total factor inputs		1.58
Residual contribution		2.91

TABLE 32

INDUSTRIAL CONTRIBUTIONS TO THE GROWTH RATE, SEVEN SECTORS, CANADA, 1937-61
(percentages)

Industry	Contribution to growth of total output	Contribution to growth of total input	Contribution to residual
Agriculture	0.21	−0.15	0.36
Forestry, fishing, trapping	0.08	0.01	0.06
Mining, quarrying, oil wells	0.29	0.12	0.17
Manufacturing	2.36	0.88	1.48
Construction	0.60	0.26	0.34
Electric power and gas utilities	0.26	0.13	0.13
Transportation, storage, communication	0.73	0.21	0.52
Total contribution	4.53	1.46	3.06

SOURCE: Table B-19.

... aggregate labour and capital inputs were computed by weighting manhours and real capital stocks in the various industry groups by the compensation per unit of labour and capital in each. ... This is a rough measure of the increasing quality of resources resulting from inter-industry transfers of resources to the extent that relative unit compensations indicate the relative marginal productivities of the resources in the various uses.

Our method of weighting inputs by industry has the distinct advantage that the productivity ratios are not affected merely by the relative shift of resources among industries—the over-all productivity index is thus conceptually an internally weighted mean of the productivity indexes for the component industries. It can be compared with the industry indexes without the necessity of explaining that part of the change in the aggregate is due to inter-industry shifts since these affect input rather than productivity by our procedure.[9]

We have not followed this procedure in immediately weighting factors in different industries because we desire an estimate of the extent of these inter-industry effects in an explicit way. Also, our use of the more complicated geometric function requires a more intricate weighting procedure. Finally, as measures of other components of quality emerge, such as on-the-job training, we would like to amend our input series to incorporate these aspects.[10] Kendrick's method includes all these components within the differences of factor compensation by industry, and hides rather than reveals their unique contributions.

CHAPTER FIVE

CONTRIBUTION OF INTER-INDUSTRY SHIFTS, UNITED STATES, 1929-57

IN THIS CHAPTER the techniques that we have developed to study growth in the Canadian economy at the industry level will be applied to the United States data to see how the performances of the two economies compare. In addition, the greater detail available for the United States allows several elaborations upon our method. These include the examination of longer run patterns, and a consideration of the effect of dealing with less aggregative units in the economy.

At the outset, our analysis parallels that of the previous chapter in scope. Thus, we consider the major components of the private domestic economy—agriculture, mining, manufacturing, construction, trade, services (which includes finance, insurance, and real estate), and a composite of transportation, communications, and public utilities. Detailed discussion of sources and methods is in Appendix C.

The period we have chosen to examine is 1929–57, in line with Denison's investigations for the total economy. The growth rates of the key variables, output, labour adjusted for quality, and net capital stock over this period are presented in Table 33. It must be pointed out that these results will not be directly comparable to our earlier adjustments of Denison's study because we are now considering only the private domestic economy, whereas Denison was studying the

TABLE 33

GROWTH RATES IN THE UNITED STATES, PRIVATE ECONOMY, 1929-57

(percentages)

Industry	Output	Labour *	Capital
Agriculture	0.94	−1.13	1.54
Mining	1.51	−0.71	−0.14
Manufacturing	3.54	1.37	2.12
Construction	2.44	1.95	†
Trade	2.68	0.93	†
Transportation, communications, public utilities	4.14	−0.20	1.32
Services	2.39	1.39	†
Aggregate	2.90	0.63	1.98

* Man-hours adjusted for changes in quality.
† Separate estimates of capital are not available. The total for these three industries can be derived (Table C-4) and it increases at 2.23 per cent per annum.

SOURCES: Output, Table C-1; Labour, Table C-2; Capital, Table C-4.

total economy. These differ only slightly from Denison's estimates for the total economy because of our omission of the government sector.[1] With these rates, it is possible to evaluate the various factor contributions to the growth rate, which are presented in Table 34.

TABLE 34

FACTOR CONTRIBUTIONS TO THE US GROWTH RATE, 1929-57

(percentages)

Industry	Labour [*]	Capital	Total factors	Residual
Agriculture	−0.97	0.22	−0.74	1.68
Mining	−0.50	−0.04	−0.54	2.05
Manufacturing	1.00	0.58	1.58	1.96
Transportation, communications, and public utilities	−0.16	0.28	0.12	4.03
Rest	1.01	0.43	1.44	0.95
Aggregate	0.49	0.46	0.94	1.96

[*] The factor coefficients used to weight the growth rates to get these contributions are the factor shares of Table C-6.

The findings in these two tables indicate at once the similarities in the two economies, and the main differences between them. A comparison of the United States performance, in the aggregate, with that of Canada suggests that our earlier findings for the total economy in both countries hold for these more limited aggregates as well.[2] In the present case, the absolute level of the factor contributions are higher in Canada, as is the residual, yielding a higher rate of growth in that country. In relative terms, there is a marked similarily, for in both countries the residual accounted for about two-thirds of the growth of output, leaving one-third to direct factor inputs. Chiefly because of higher quality, labour in the United States is more important than capital, whereas the reverse holds true for Canada. In fact, the capital contribution in Canada is almost twice that in the United States in absolute terms because of the very high capital growth rates which we have observed in Table 7. Thus we arrive at the same conclusion which we came to in the second chapter; an examination of the differences in the growth rates of the two countries must, in addition to explaining the different performances of labour and capital, show why the residuals in the two countries behaved so differently.

As we have argued earlier, the residual is composed of the intra-industry growth in productivity and inter-industry shifts of the factors of production. The former process will be considered next, after which we shall evaluate the impact of inter-industry shifts in the United States' growth.

In agriculture, the growth rate of the residual is very similar in the two economies.[3] The higher rate of growth of output in Canada has been due to the very rapid rate of capital accumulation, making capital's contribution there more than four times as large as that of capital in the United States (see Table 15). This was sufficient to offset the greater reduction of agricultural labour input in Canada, thereby allowing the direct factor input in that country to decline at only half the United States rate.

In mining, the growth rate of the residual in the United States once again is very close to the Canadian growth rate. However, the difference in the growth rate of output in this sector is particularly striking. In Canada, the mining industry has been, over the period under discussion, one of the most dynamic of all, attracting vast amounts of capital, in large part from the United States. On the contrary, in the United States this same industry has grown at a rate one-half of that of the total economy, making mining a declining industry. What is happening, in effect, is a shift of the locus of this industry from the United States to Canada, made possible by the great mobility of capital between the two countries.[4] This accounts for the very impressive performance of mining in Canada, particularly with respect to the high level of capital accumulation which contributed almost 60 per cent to the growth rate of output. The fact that labour's role in this industry is so small in both economies has greatly augmented the ability of mining to shift to rich raw material sites even though these occur across national boundaries.

The manufacturing industries in the two countries display similar growth patterns. Whereas the absolute level of the factor and residual contributions are higher in Canada, their relative roles are quite similar, with the residual about one-half the growth rate in Canada, and more than one-half in the United States. Labour has played a slightly greater role relative to capital in Canada, but both factors are absolutely greater, in terms of their contribution to the growth rate, in the Canadian manufacturing sector.

In both Canada and the United States, transportation, communications, and public utilities have shown rates of growth considerably in excess of the aggregate. This has been due largely to the very high residual contribution within these industries. This sector is unique in that the American residual is absolutely greater than the Canadian. The higher growth rate of output in these sectors in Canada is due, consequently, to the much greater factor contributions, with labour predominant in transportation, and capital in utilities. In the United States, the negative labour contribution and the rather small capital contribution have led to a very slight factor contribution. An inquiry into the nature of this residual which has been of overwhelming importance would add greatly to our understanding of growth in this industry in the United States as well as in Canada.

The remaining sectors cannot be individually compared because we have had to combine them for the United States. It is possible to compare their growth rates, however, which leads to several interesting observations. The first is that the construction industries in the two countries have been characterized by labour inputs that have grown at rates far surpassing the national average. Trade and services, including finance, insurance, and real estate, have also shown large growth rates of labour input. The lower-than-average growth rate of output in these industries suggests that the residual contribution has been much smaller than in other industries, as was found for the Canadian economy. However, the much higher growth rate of capital input in these industries in Canada has likely resulted in a higher level of factor contributions, explaining in part the higher growth rate of output. It is not possible to infer the absolute size of the individual residuals in the United States, however, without the necessary capital stock data. Taken together, their residual is far below that of any of the other industries. The same holds true for Canada, with the exception of the construction industry.

From this analysis of comparative economic growth at the industrial level, several generalizations emerge. Growth in Canada has consisted of larger doses of both capital and labour. However, the growth of the intra-industry residuals has been marked by a great amount of similarity. Thus, the greater rate of growth in the Canadian industries is due to the more important role of the direct factors of production.

The similarity of the residuals at the intra-industry level leaves unanswered our original problem, which was the very great discrepancy in the growth rate of the aggregate residuals. Our earlier analysis of the second element in the aggregate residual—the effect of inter-industry shifts of the factors of production—suggests a possible answer to this otherwise inexplicable dilemma. For if the industries within the two economies show the same amount of intra-industry productivity advance, how else is the divergence of such major proportions likely to come about in the aggregate residuals?

The measurement of inter-industry shifts follows the same procedure as was developed in the preceding chapter. The basic data are presented in the Appendix and we consider in Table 35 only the information required for the final step in the calculation.

TABLE 35

THE MEASUREMENT OF INTER-INDUSTRY SHIFTS, US, 1929-57

Industry	Weights	Share in labour		Share in total output	
		1929	1957	1929	1957
	$	%	%	%	%
Agriculture	0.37	22.28	11.86	19.70	10.93
Mining	0.90	2.02	1.34	2.27	1.45
Manufacturing	0.90	21.26	26.32	23.64	28.12
Construction	0.65	4.64	6.73	*	*
Trade	0.66	20.60	22.55	*	*
Transportation, communications, public utilities	1.62	9.15	7.29	9.02	7.16
Services	0.91	20.05	23.92	*	*

* The combined share of these three industries in total factor input was 45.37 per cent in 1929 and 52.34 per cent in 1957.

SOURCES: Weights, Table C-6; Shares in total input measured in labour equivalents, Table C-2; Shares in total input, Table C-7.

The effect of the shifts, under the assumption of complementarity and substitution, are summarized in Table 36. For the complementarity case, we measure shifts for the seven industries; for five, where construction, trade, and services have been combined; and for four, where these have been omitted altogether, making the analysis comparable with the seven sector Canadian study contained in Tables 28 through 32. The substitution case contains the measures of shifts for the five- and the four-industry groupings only.

The grouping of the construction, trade, and service industries into one sector has apparently had very little effect on the inter-industry term, for in the complementarity case, it reduced the term by 0.005 percentage points, or by about 3½ per cent. The same bias from grouping applied to the substitution case would raise the term from 0.107 to 0.110 percentage points, clearly a very slight improvement. In Table 37 we present the adjustment for the inter-industry effect, and compare the resultant residual with that of Canada for a comparable industrial grouping. In both cases, we are employing the substitution assumption.

TABLE 36

CROWTH OF OUTPUT FROM INTER-INDUSTRY SHIFTS, US, 1929-57
(percentages)

Industry grouping	Complementarity	Substitution
Seven sectors	0.15	—
Five sectors *	0.14	0.11
Four sectors †	0.32	0.25

* Construction, trade, and services taken together.
† The above three omitted.

TABLE 37

SOURCES OF CROWTH, US AND CANADA, PRIVATE DOMESTIC ECONOMY
(percentages)

	US (five sectors)		Canada (ten sectors)
Growth rate of output		2.90	4.54
Direct factor inputs:			
Labour	0.49		0.65
Capital	0.46		0.82
	0.95		1.47
Indirect inputs (from shifts)	0.11		0.66
Total factor inputs		1.05	2.13
Residual contribution		1.85	2.41

SOURCE: Table 26 for Canada.

The sharp difference in the size of the inter-industry term in the two economies explains the problem which has been puzzling us. With that effect now accounted for, the proximity of the residuals is in line with our expectations, given our findings for the individual industries. The reason for Canada's much higher inter-industry effect will be considered as soon as we have made several tests of the United States results. The first is a comparison of the four sector case with the similar restricted case for Canada (Table 38).

Once again the discrepancy in the simple residual term is largely explained by the inter-industry terms. The net United States residual can be tested in the same way as were the Canadian residuals in Table 27. The results of this test are given in Table 39.

Comparing these findings with the results of Table 37 again indicates that our adjustment has been necessary to reflect the relative orders of magnitude of the various factor contributions to growth. We are now in a position to compare the revised residual contributions in the two countries in order to determine the reasons for Canada's much greater gains from inter-industry shifts, for it is this element, in conjunction with the greater role of the measured factors of production, labour, and capital, that explains the higher rate of economic growth in Canada.

Much of the inter-industry effect derives from the exodus of labour from agriculture into sectors where its productivity was considerably higher. During the

TABLE 38

SOURCES OF GROWTH, US AND CANADA, LIMITED AGGREGATES
(percentages)

	US (four sectors)		Canada (seven sectors)
Growth rate of output		3.23	4.49
Direct factor inputs:			
Labour	0.03		−0.24
Capital	0.37		0.86
	0.40		0.62
Indirect inputs (from shifts)	0.25		0.96
Total factor inputs		0.65	1.58
Residual contribution		2.58	2.91

SOURCE: Table 31 for Canada.

TABLE 39

INDUSTRIAL CONTRIBUTIONS TO US GROWTH, LIMITED AGGREGATES, 1929-57
(percentages)

Industry	Contribution to growth of total output	Contribution to growth of total input	Contribution to residual
Agriculture	0.07	−0.14	0.21
Mining	0.03	−0.01	0.04
Manufacturing	1.08	0.44	0.64
Transportation, communications, public utilities	0.67	0.01	0.66
Rest	1.15	0.70	0.45
Total contribution	3.00	1.01	2.00

SOURCE: Table C-8.

period under consideration, 1937-61, this occurred at a relatively greater speed than did the same process in the United States. Table 24 indicates that in Canada, the share of agriculture in standardized labour input declined from 41 to 15 per cent in these twenty-four years, while in the United States, the decline over a longer period, 1929-57, was less, falling from 22 to 12 per cent (see Table 35). In the United States, this declining role of agriculture was made up by similar increases in manufacturing and in services. In Canada, the gain by the service industries is almost twice the gain in manufacturing. The result of these differential impacts has been a very great similarity in the distribution of labour input by industry in the two economies, from a position of greater dissimilarity several decades earlier. This does not hold for the distribution of total factor input by industry, where agriculture is much more prominent in Canada, and manufacturing is larger in the total in the United States (Tables 25 and 35).

Insofar as the shift out of agriculture has been the key to Canada's greater gain from inter-industry effects, it is necessary to consider the longer run possibilities of this element as a contributor to growth. Obviously the trend cannot continue indefinitely; but it is also very likely that the shift cannot continue at the same rate even in the near future. This is due to Canada's comparative advantage in growing such export staples as wheat, together with the need to supply a rapidly growing population with basic dietary needs.

If this is the case, this specific source of growth cannot be as large in the future. The experience of the United States tends to substantiate this prognosis, for in that country, the exodus from agriculture in the recent period has occurred at a much slower pace than in Canada, because of the great shift much earlier. As a result, the inter-industry effect has been much less important as a contributor to growth in the recent past.

One particularly interesting by-product of this study is the discovery of a great deal of similarity of the intra-industry residuals in the two economies. This implies very similar productivity advance at the industry level, which arises from the very great interdependence that exists between these two nations. Most significant in this respect have been the extreme mobility of capital and the free flow of ideas. Since capital incorporates a great number of technological improvements, the international transfer of capital goods is significant in making the residual contributions similar. As for the free flow of ideas, they affect the structure of production both from the supply side and the demand side, where the fashioning of similar tastes appears as a most important element.

With the more comprehensive quantitative description of growth available for the United States, it is possible to refine the present analysis in two dimensions. The first is a broadening of the framework within which inter-industry effects are measured, and the second is an expansion of the temporal horizon to observe the characteristics of long-run economic growth in that country. The former task

TABLE 40
INTER-INDUSTRY SHIFTS WITHIN MANUFACTURING, US, 1929-57

Subsector	Weights	Shares in labour		Shares in total input measured in labour equivalents	
		1929	1957	1929	1957
	$	%	%	%	%
Food	0.81	10.66	9.09	11.16	8.93
Textiles	0.74	18.99	12.25	18.81	10.86
Leather	0.81	3.52	2.02	2.96	1.52
Rubber	0.88	1.73	1.76	1.61	1.51
Forest products	0.71	9.81	5.39	8.96	4.65
Paper	0.70	3.18	3.56	3.57	4.01
Printing	1.18	5.98	5.14	5.08	4.28
Chemicals	1.39	3.56	5.46	3.91	7.97
Petroleum	1.24	1.42	1.33	2.60	3.35
Stone, clay	0.84	3.80	3.71	4.40	3.67
Primary metals	1.05	7.18	6.99	6.88	7.73
Fabricated metals	0.79	6.54	8.73	5.88	8.33
Non-electric machinery	0.76	10.24	12.90	10.97	12.89
Electrical machinery	1.17	4.48	6.88	4.27	6.20
Transport equipment	0.79	6.27	11.37	6.47	11.04
Miscellany, instruments	1.23	2.63	3.41	2.46	3.07

SOURCES: Weights, Table D-5, Labour shares, Table D-1; Shares in total input, Table D-6.

is based upon the possibility of dealing with the major subsectors of manufacturing, for which the necessary information is readily available. These data and their sources are described in Appendix D. Table 40 sets out the distribution of inputs necessary for the measurements of inter-industry shifts within the manufacturing sector.

The effect of shifts among the subsectors of manufacturing would have ac-counted for 0.17 percentage points under the substitution assumption. Within manufacturing, therefore, the sources of growth would be as described in Table 41.

TABLE 41

SOURCES OF GROWTH IN MANUFACTURING, US, 1929-57

(percentages)

Growth rate of output		3.54
Direct factor inputs:		
Labour	1.00	
Capital	0.58	
	1.58	
Indirect inputs (from shifts)	0.17	
Total factor inputs		1.76
Residual contribution		1.78

This shift is seen to be of some importance within the manufacturing sector, amounting to about one-tenth of the intra-subsectoral growth in productivity. The impact if this shift on the aggregate residual is less marked, because of the influence of the other sectors, as can be seen in Table 42.

TABLE 42

INTER-INDUSTRY SHIFTS, INCLUDING SUBSECTORS OF MANUFACTURING, US, 1929-57

(percentages)

Industry grouping *	Complementarity	Substitution
Seven sectors:		
Without subsectors of manufacturing	0.15	—
Including subsectors	0.17	—
Five sectors:		
Without subsectors of manufacturing	0.14	0.11
Including subsectors	0.16	0.15
Four sectors:		
Without subsectors of manufacturing	0.32	0.25
Including subsectors	0.36	0.34
Manufacturing only:	0.10	0.17

* See Table 36 for industries in the sectoral groupings.

Including this new shift component in our allocation of the sources of growth in the United States results in the contributions presented in Table 43. The effect of including this item is substantial, raising the inter-industry term based on the substitution assumption by almost one-half. The impact on the aggregate residual is small, however, because of the minor part played by these shifts in the United States during the period 1929–57.

TABLE 43

SOURCES OF GROWTH, US, 1929-57,
SHIFTS WITHIN MANUFACTURING INCLUDED

	Five sectors	Four sectors
Growth rate of output	2.90	3.23
Direct factor inputs:		
Labour	0.49	0.03
Capital	0.46	0.37
	0.94	0.40
Indirect inputs (all shifts)	0.15	0.34
Total factor inputs	1.09	0.34
Residual contribution	1.81	2.49

A recent study of manufacturing in Canada reveals that shifts within manufacturing would have reduced the aggregate net residual by 0.07 points as compared to the 0.05 percentage point reduction in the United States. This would lower the growth rate of the Canadian residual to 2.34 per cent, marginally closer to that of the United States.[5]

This analysis suggests that still further dis-aggregation may have important consequences for the inter-industry term. We have already found that the difference between the five sector grouping and the more detailed seven sector grouping is negligible with respect to the size of the inter-industry term. However, another form of dis-aggregation, which goes to the level of the firm, may yield entirely surprising results. It is impossible to carry the present analysis to that stage, and we are left, therefore, with a word of caution; all the shifts in industrial structure have not been accounted for by this analysis. Only further research will reveal the magnitude of the omission and the direction of its impact.

TABLE 44

GROWTH RATES IN MANUFACTURING, US, 1929-57
(percentages)

Subsector	Output	Labour	Capital
Food	3.07	0.80	0.50
Textiles	1.98	-0.19	-0.73
Leather	0.81	-0.54	-1.50
Rubber	2.92	1.44	0.73
Forest products	1.57	-0.64	-0.84
Paper	3.97	1.78	2.17
Printing	2.42	0.83	1.14
Chemicals	6.69	2.94	5.57
Petroleum	3.72	1.14	3.04
Stone, clay	3.21	1.29	0.06
Primary metals	2.43	1.28	3.24
Fabricated metals	3.85	2.43	3.77
Non-electric machinery	3.77	2.22	1.84
Electrical machinery	6.00	2.94	2.66
Transport equipment	4.66	3.56	3.25
Miscellany, instruments	4.57	2.37	2.24

SOURCES: Output, Kendrick, *Productivity Trends in the United States*, 468-75, Table D-IV; Labour, Table D-1; Capital, Table D-3.

It is useful to examine the nature of growth within the particular subsectors of manufacturing, in order to relate the observed trends to the changes in factor shares. Weighting to growth rates in Table 44 by the factor coefficients given in Appendix Table D-5 gives the factor contributions to the growth of output within each of the subsectors of manufacturing (Table 45).

TABLE 45

FACTOR CONTRIBUTIONS TO THE GROWTH OF MANUFACTURING OUTPUT, US, 1929-57
(percentages)

Subsector	Contributions of			Residual
	Labour	Capital	Total factors	
Food	0.58	0.13	0.72	2.36
Textiles	−0.15	−0.16	−0.30	2.28
Leather	−0.47	−0.18	−0.65	1.46
Rubber	1.14	0.15	1.29	1.62
Forest products	−0.52	−0.16	−0.68	2.25
Paper	1.19	0.72	1.91	2.06
Printing	0.68	0.20	0.88	1.54
Chemicals	1.81	2.13	3.95	2.74
Petroleum	0.37	2.06	2.43	1.29
Stone, clay	0.97	0.02	0.99	2.29
Primary metals	0.92	0.92	1.84	0.59
Fabricated metals	1.87	0.87	2.74	1.11
Non-electric machinery	1.69	0.44	2.13	1.64
Electrical machinery	2.28	0.60	2.87	3.12
Transport equipment	2.51	0.95	3.47	1.16
Miscellany, instruments	1.91	0.44	2.35	2.22

Using Spearman's rank correlation test to discover the nature of the relationships involved, we find that there is very strong, positive correlation between the various factor contributions and the growth rate, with the exception of the residual. These are summarized in Table 46.

TABLE 46

RANK CORRELATION TEST OF KEY FACTORS IN GROWTH OF MANUFACTURING, US, 1929-57

Correlation between	r_s	Significance level
		%
Labour contribution and the growth rate of output	0.88	99.95
Capital contribution and the growth rate of output	0.73	99.50
Residual and the growth rate of output	0.20	nil
Residual and the total factor contribution	−0.09	nil

Using the same test to relate the extent of changes in the distribution of factor inputs to the growth of output and to the growth of the residual gives the results set out in Table 47. It appears that there is no association between the size of the residual and the change in industrial structure. However, the strong positive relationship between the growth rate and both the factor contributions and the change in the distribution of factors of production suggests that rapidly growing industries draw on factors of production very heavily, altering thereby the distribution of inputs in their favour. Thus the two fastest growing subsectors of manufacturing, chemical products and electric machinery, have increased their

TABLE 47

RELATIONSHIP OF CHANGES IN FACTOR SHARES TO RELEVANT VARIABLES,
US MANUFACTURING, 1929-57

Correlation between	r_R	Significance level
		%
Change in shares of total factors and the growth rate	0.81	99.95
Change in shares of total factors and the residual	−0.27	nil

share both in labour and total factor input very substantially, while the slower growing textile, leather, and forest product industries have undergone major declines in their share of inputs.

Our conclusion, therefore, for the manufacturing industries is that the most rapidly growing industries were instrumental in altering the basic factor distribution, but this rapid growth was not uniquely based on greater intra-industry productivity advance.

CHAPTER SIX

LONG TERM GROWTH IN CANADA AND THE UNITED STATES SINCE 1890

AT THE OUTSET of this chapter, we shall make use of the abundant United States data to examine the nature of long-term changes in the industrial structure in that country. Following this, we shall contrast the performance of the aggregate economy in Canada and the United States.

The years selected for the long-run analysis of United States industrial structure are 1889 and 1909 in addition to the more recent years, 1929 and 1957. These are all years of high level economic activity, and are close to census years upon which our quality adjustments are based. The sources of the text material are to be found in Appendix E-I.

From Appendix Table E-5, we are able to compute the inter-industry effects

TABLE 48

GROWTH OF OUTPUT RESULTING FROM INTER-INDUSTRY SHIFTS, LONG RUN, US

(percentages)

Period	Assumption	Seven sectors	Five sectors	Four sectors
1889-1909	Complementarity	0.31	0.30	0.48
	substitution	°	0.28	0.46
1909-29	Complementarity	-0.06	-0.05	-0.04
	substitution	°	0.01	0.03
1929-57	Complementarity	0.15	0.14	0.32
	substitution	°	0.11	0.25

° Data do not permit this calculation.

TABLE 49

LONG-RUN GROWTH RATES, US, 1889-1957

(percentages)

	Output	Labour	Capital
Five sector group:			
1889-1909	4.24	2.59	4.67
1909-29	3.11	1.54	2.56
1929-57	2.90	0.63	1.98
Four sector group:			
1889-1909	3.64	2.42	3.62
1909-29	3.23	0.94	2.33
1929-57	3.23	0.04	1.55

SOURCES: Output, Projection of 1929 output estimates of Table C-5 (1) by indexes given in Kendrick, *Productivity Trends in the United States*, 302-3, Table A-IV; Labour, Tables E-2 and C-2; Capital, Tables E-3 and C-4.

under the two assumptions of complementarity and substitution, using the various groupings indicated in Table 36. These are given in Table 48. The final step in this analysis is to see how these shifts in industrial structure affect the sources of economic growth.

To derive these, we require the growth rates of the variables, which are given in Table 49.

Weighting these growth rates of labour and capital by their respective co-efficients allows us to calculate the factor contributions to the growth rate in each period.[1] These are summarized in Table 50, where the inter-industry terms are also taken into account.

TABLE 50

Sources of Long-Run Economic Growth, US

(percentages)

	1889-1909		1909-29		1929-57 °	
Five sectors						
Growth rate of output		4.24		3.11		2.90
Direct factor inputs:						
Labour	1.68		1.07		0.49	
Capital	1.63		0.78		0.46	
	3.32		1.85		0.94	
Indirect inputs (from shifts)	0.28		−0.01		0.11	
Total factor inputs		3.59		1.84		1.05
Residual contribution		0.65		1.27		1.85
Four sectors						
Growth rate of output		3.65		3.23		3.23
Direct factor inputs:						
Labour	1.72		0.69		0.03	
Capital	1.05		0.63		0.37	
	2.77		1.32		0.40	
Indirect inputs (from shifts)	0.46		0.03		0.25	
Total factor inputs		3.23		1.34		0.65
Residual contribution		0.42		1.89		2.58

° From Tables 37 and 38.

Table 50 contains a great deal of information on the changing characteristics of United States economic growth. The deceleration of the growth rate has been due chiefly to the declining contributions of labour and capital, which were only one-third that of the earliest period by 1929-57. The decline of capital's role was most prominent in the 1909-29 period, while the labour contribution fell relatively less than capital's in the middle period, and more in the most recent one.

The pattern of inter-industry shifts over time also displays unexpected charac-teristics. The relatively high contribution of this item in 1889-1909 is missing during the middle period, and is only partially regained in the latest years. The

very high level is due to the shift out of agriculture into industries with very high
weights, such as manufacturing, mining, services, transportation, communications,
and public utilities. Between 1909 and 1929, the shift out of agriculture was much
smaller, and the gains went to the lower productivity industries, such as trade,
while mining, transportation, communications, and public utilities declined somewhat in their share of inputs, and manufacturing remained relatively unchanged.
The later period witnessed a very large shift out of agriculture once more—the
low productivity industries gaining most, mining, transportation, communications,
and public utilities declining still further, but with some offset being provided by
the gain in the share of manufacturing—yielding a positive inter-industry term,
but a smaller one than that of the earliest period as can be seen by comparing
Tables 35 and 52.

The effect of these direct and indirect factor contributions has been to arrest the
total factor contribution, the rate of decline being about 50 per cent from one
period to the following. This has led to an ever-increasing role for the intra-
industry growth in productivity, which almost doubled between the first period and
the second, and increased by another 50 per cent from the second to the third.
This latter deceleration was insufficient to offset the declining role of the factor
inputs even though these latter were bolstered by a positive inter-industry term.
The findings for the more limited four sector grouping largely substantiate these
conclusions, with only slight variations in the orders of magnitude.

With regard to the Canadian results, our pessimism as to the future gain from
shifts out of agriculture seems to be warranted. The early large impact was never
attained again in the United States, although one of the main reasons for this has
been the changing direction of the shift. If the present trend in Canada of shifting
only slightly into manufacturing, transportation, storage, communications, and
much more extensively into services and trade continues, there is no reason to
doubt that the inter-industry effect will slacken (see Tables 24 and 25). This
supports our earlier comments about the limited scope for a reduction of inputs
in agriculture.

With the trend in direct factor inputs distinctly falling, with only limited assistance forthcoming from shifts in the industrial structure, the burden of increasing or even of maintaining the growth rate falls on two elements. The first
is productivity advance, based on the advance of knowledge and its effective

TABLE 51

LONG-RUN GROWTH RATES BY INDUSTRY, US

(percentages)

Industry	1889-1909			1909-29			1929-57		
	Output	Labour	Capital	Output	Labour	Capital	Output	Labour	Capital
Agriculture	1.48	1.35	2.79	0.80	0.85	1.03	0.94	−1.13	1.54
Mining	5.57	3.72	6.60	3.00	0.39	4.34	1.51	−0.71	−0.14
Manufacturing	4.41	3.30	5.80	4.26	1.31	3.09	3.54	1.37	2.12
Transportation, etc.	5.71	3.35	3.04	3.98	0.50	2.28	4.14	−0.20	1.32
Rest	5.08	2.87	5.43	3.00	2.39	2.68	2.39	1.46	2.23

SOURCES: Output, Kendrick, *Productivity Trends in the United States*, 302-3, Table A-IV;
Labour, Tables E-2 and C-2; Capital, Tables E-3 and C-4.

application. In addition, and related most intimately with it, is the improvement in the quality of the labour force, particularly from education, but also from the reduction of discrimination in its many guises.[2]

In addition to these trends of the aggregative variables, we can observe the changing growth patterns within the various sectors. Table 51 summarizes the growth rates of output, labour, and capital in the various industries in the United States over the long run. The factor coefficients by industry are contained in Appendix E-I. Weighting the above growth rates by these gives the various factor contributions to the growth of output in each industry (Table 52).

TABLE 52

FACTOR CONTRIBUTIONS TO THE LONG-RUN GROWTH RATE, BY INDUSTRY, US
(percentages)

| Industry | Contributions of | | | Residual |
	Labour	Capital	Total	
1889-1909				
Agriculture	0.85	1.03	1.86	−0.41 *
Mining	2.60	1.98	4.58	0.99
Manufacturing	2.53	1.35	3.88	0.65
Transportation	2.49	0.78	3.27	2.44
Rest	1.87	1.90	3.77	1.31
1909-29				
Agriculture	0.48	0.45	0.93	−0.13 *
Mining	0.27	1.30	1.57	1.43
Manufacturing	1.00	0.72	1.72	2.54
Transportation	0.38	0.56	0.93	3.05
Rest	1.66	0.82	2.48	0.52
1929-57				
Agriculture	−0.97	0.22	−0.74	1.68
Mining	−0.50	−0.04	−0.54	2.05
Manufacturing	1.00	0.58	1.58	1.96
Transportation	−0.16	0.28	0.12	4.03
Rest	1.01	0.43	1.44	0.95

* The negative sign is due to the limited scope of the capital concept. With land and inventories, the growth rate would have been 1.62 and 0.53 per cent for capital, giving a capital contribution of 0.60 and 0.23 percentage points and a residual of 0.03 and 0.09 percentage points.

We see that throughout the sixty-eight years under consideration agriculture has been the slowest growing industry. The labour contribution has steadily declined until, in the latest period, it was negative and rather large. The capital contribution has also diminished, though at a less drastic pace. This has meant that the total factor contribution in the sector has likewise fallen steadily. The much milder decline in the growth rate of output is due, consequently, to an impressive increase in the residual's contribution.

The mining industry has fallen from one of the fastest growing in 1889-1909 to next to the slowest in 1929-57. With labour's contribution falling sharply, with capital also contributing a smaller amount, the decline in total factor input has been the main element in the slowing down of the growth rate in this industry.

The residual contribution has increased substantially, however, almost doubling in absolute size so that by the most recent period, it grew faster than output itself.

Manufacturing grew at almost the same rate over the first two periods, with a slackening of the rate occurring in the years 1929-57. Once more the labour contribution has fallen, but the decline from the second to the third period has been very slight. Similarly, the decline in the capital contribution was greater from the earliest to the second period. This has given the total factor input decline the same pattern. In contrast, the residual in manufacturing rose very sharply from 1889–1909 to 1909–29, but declined slightly from the latter to the most recent period. Thus, it is this dual decline in both total factors and in the residual that has led to the slowing down of the growth rate of manufacturing output in the years 1929-57.

Transportation, communications, and public utilities have been the fastest growing of all the sectors, with the highest rate being attained in the earliest period, a rather sharp drop following in the next period, and a slight recovery of the rate during 1929–57. Thus the general decline in labour and capital contributions has been largely offset by the very high and increasing residual contribution.

The final sector, which includes services, finance and related industries, trade, and construction has also undergone a steady decline in the level of its growth rate. However, the decline in the labour contribution is much less than in the other sectors, and is largely centred on the latest period. The capital contribution is cut in half over each of the successive periods, and its total decline is therefore much greater than that of labour. The over-all result is a decline in total factor input that is accompanied by a sharp fall in the residual contribution from the first to the second period, with only a partial recovery thereafter.

The broad patterns in these individual industries help to explain our findings for the total economy. We see that the intra-industry advance in productivity has not been confined to any one industry, but that its acceleration has marked the progress of all sectors with the exception of the last, rather heterogeneous one. The decline in factor inputs has likewise occurred in all the industries, although the timing has shown some variation both as to the individual factors of production, and the total factor item itself. Thus, the long-term trends that have characterized aggregate economic growth have also taken place within the various key sectors of the economy. The general decline in growth rates has been due to the sharp falling off of the various factor contributions, and this has not been offset by intra-industry productivity advances. However, inter-industry shifts during the latest period did succeed in almost maintaining the growth rate of the preceding period (see Table 50).

It is interesting to note that there is no significant relationship between the rate of growth of output and the extent of changes in the distribution of factor inputs. This contrasts with the pattern observed in the manufacturing subsectors, and is largely due to the shift of factors to the service industries, which are among the slower growing ones. In addition, there is little relationship between the rate of growth and the intra-industry growth in productivity, which held also for the manufacturing industries. Since these results are found for each of the three time periods, it is possible to generalize, making the results descriptive of the nature of growth in the United States over the entire sixty-eight year span.

The Canadian data do not permit as refined an analysis as the foregoing for the longer time span. However, it is possible to observe the general patterns of growth in the total economy. The necessary estimation procedures which have been followed are given in Appendix E-II.

In Table 53, we observe that the growth of output in Canada has differed considerably from that in the United States (Table 50). In the United States, the initial rate was particularly high, surpassing any growth rate ever attained in Canada. However, there has been a significant deceleration in the growth rate in the United States over the long run, while in Canda the low rate of the 1910-26 period was followed by a record high rate of growth, so that it was almost one-third greater than that of the United States in the final period.

TABLE 53

Long-Run Growth Rates, Canada, 1891-1956

(percentages)

Period	Output	Labour*	Capital
1891-1910	3.38	2.31	3.82
1910-1926	2.46	1.25	1.47
1926-1956	3.89	0.77	2.86

* Labour includes only man-hours here, as the data required for the quality adjustments are inadequate. The US data indicate that these are not too significant at the aggregate level.

SOURCES: Output, Firestone, *Canada's Economic Development*, 276, Table 87; Capital, Table E-7; Labour, Table E-6.

The causes of these patterns of growth can be evaluated by considering the various factor contributions. To do so, we require estimates of the factor coefficients prior to 1926. Unfortunately the available data do not permit their estimation. The coefficients that relate to the entire period 1926-56 have been used as the best alternative for the early years. It should be noted that this may introduce a slight bias into our factor contribution estimates if the experience of the United States, with a slight increase in the labour coefficient over time, holds for Canada

TABLE 54

Sources of Long-Run Growth, Canada, 1891-1956

(percentages)

	1891-1910		1910-1926		1926-1956	
Growth rate of output		3.38		2.46		3.89
Direct factor inputs:						
Labour	1.82		0.98		0.58	
Capital	0.81		0.31		0.61	
		2.63		1.30		1.18
Residual contribution *		0.75		1.16		2.70

* No separation of inter-industry effects has been made. The comparable residuals in Table 50 are 0.92, 1.26, and 1.96.

as well. The order of magnitude of this bias is likely very small, however, and no serious distortion of the findings should arise (Table 54).

The previous analysis for the United States is not directly comparable with the present one for Canada. For the measurement of inter-industry shifts, we considered the private domestic economy, whereas we are now considering the national economy. Also, we present our labour input in man-hours without further refinement, for Canada, while the United States data were adjusted for quality changes. Thus, it is necessary to present comparable United States data if the two economies are to be contrasted. Table 55 presents the revised growth rates in the United States.

TABLE 55

LONG-RUN GROWTH RATES, US, NATIONAL ECONOMY

(percentages)

Period	Output	Labour [*]	Capital [†]
1889-1909	4.23	2.26	4.78
1909-1929	3.17	1.22	2.74
1929-1957	2.95	0.53	1.01

[*] Man-hours only.
[†] Machinery, equipment, and construction in prices of 1929.
SOURCES: Kendrick, *Productivity Trends in the United States*: Output, 298-300, Table A-III; Labour, 311-3, Table A-X; Capital, 323-5, Table A-XVI.

With the coefficients given by Kendrick for the national economy,[3] it is possible to evaluate the various factor contributions. These are summarized in Table 56 where there is no significant alteration of the results found in Table 50, except for the slightly larger labour contribution in the latter because of the quality adjustments. We see in both economies a continuous decline in the labour contribution, of about the same proportions, with the level of its contribution in Canada above that in the United States throughout the period.

TABLE 56

SOURCES OF LONG-RUN GROWTH, US, NATIONAL ECONOMY

(percentages)

	1889-1909		1909-1929		1929-1957	
Growth rate of output		4.23		3.17		2.95
Direct factor inputs:						
Labour	1.45		0.83		0.41	
Capital	1.72		0.86		0.23	
		3.17		1.70		0.64
Residual contribution [*]		1.07		1.48		2.31

[*] Inter-industry effects have not been separated from the residual.

The role of capital is entirely different in the two economies. The continual decline of this element in the United States results in a capital contribution in 1929-57 of about one-eighth its earliest period contribution. In Canada, the level of the capital contribution in the early period was only one-half that in the United States, but the sharp decline in the middle period was largely reversed in the final one, so that the capital contribution in the last period was absolutely above that in the United States.

Thus the roles played by the factors of production have varied significantly over the long run in the two countries. While both labour and capital were absolutely of greater importance in the United States than in Canada in the early period, the sharp decline in their impact in the former country contrasts sharply with their much more moderate fall in Canada, so that by the 1926-56 period, the absolute level of their contribution was higher in Canada.

The comparison of the residuals is particularly instructive. From the first to the second period, a moderate rise in this item can be observed for both countries. The level of the United States residual is above that of Canada in both these periods, most probably because of the differential timing of inter-industry shifts. We have already noted that, in the United States, the greatest impact of these shifts occurred during 1889-1909. While there is no way of accurately measuring the extent of these shifts in Canada prior to 1937, a rough calculation of the effect of shifts of the Canadian labour force alone does indicate that the earlier shifts were less significant than the most recent ones. Therefore, it is very likely that part of the higher United States residual in these years was due to greater gains arising from changes in the industrial structure. In the most recent period, the two economies showed very sharp increases in their residuals, with the increase in Canda far surpassing that in the United States. As we have earlier concluded, most of this differential is due to Canada's much greater gain from inter-industry shifts in this period.

With these results, it is possible to explain the differences in the patterns of the growth rates in the two economies. The higher rate in the United States in the first period was due almost entirely to the greater capital contribution, with some added impact of the greater residual arising from a larger inter-industry effect. These factors explain the same margin of the United States growth rate over the Canadian in the second period. During the final period, Canada's higher growth rate was due both to its greater factor contribution and to its significantly greater residual, with the margin between the two residuals being largely explained by Canada's inter-industry shifts.

Even disregarding these shifts, there has been, throughout the entire period, an acceleration of the intra-industry productivity component. This has been accompanied by a falling off of direct factor inputs in both countries, and some very interesting questions of causation are thereby raised.

It may be argued that the slowing down of factor inputs has been caused by the growth in productivity. This would come about if innovations served to raise factor productivity and if some of this gain were taken in the form of more leisure, in the case of labour, and greater consumption with lower saving on the part of owners of capital. Conversely, the growth in productivity may have been due to a decline in the rate of growth of factor supplies, which would operate to raise factor costs and stimulate innovation as an offset. In the case of labour, this might be due to a decline in the growth of the labour force itself, because of a variety of demographic and cultural factors. Among the former, the rate of natural increase and the extent of migration should be considered, while the latter is concerned with such things as participation rates, discrimination against certain members of the population, and the like. In addition, shifts in the preference functions of members of the labour force towards more leisure would produce the same effect. As for capital, an increase in the propensity to consume, or the channelling of domestic savings abroad would serve to raise the domestic supply price of capital, and stimulate capital saving innovations.

In practice, it is particularly difficult to separate cause and effect, because the events would be accompanied by similar economic phenomena, such as rising factor prices and a decline in the average number of hours worked per week. Furthermore, it is unrealistic to presume that there is a single direction of causation. Rather, the situation is composed of continuous interaction of these processes, and no statistical technique is available for assigning numerical values to their relative importance.

Our modest conclusion is that there appears to be a strong relationship of substitution between productivity advance and the growth of factor input at the aggregate level over time, with the decline in factor input being more than offset in Canada, thereby raising its growth rate of output, and with the offset in the United States being insufficient to compensate for the very rapid decline in direct factor input, with the result that the growth rate has been secularly declining.

It is possible to examine these conclusions in the light of the growth experience of the Norwegian economy over an extended period of time. Most of the data are given in Bjerke's study, and the years are selected from his choices of peak years.[4] The relevant growth rates are given in the following table.

TABLE 57

LONG-RUN GROWTH RATES, NORWAY, 1877-1956
(percentages)

Period	Output	Labour [*]	Capital
1877-1899	1.72	0.68	1.87
1899-1930	2.76	0.20	2.34
1930-1956	2.85	0.32	2.62

[*] Man-hours only.
SOURCES: Output, Bjerke, *Some Aspects of Long-Term Economic Growth of Norway Since 1865*, GDP, 28, Table IV.2. Capital, *ibid.*, from decadal capital-output ratios of Table IV.5 (3). 36; Labour force, *ibid.*, 17, Table II.6, Hours were taken from Colin Clark, *The Conditions of Economic Progress*, 3rd ed. (Toronto. 1957). 174-5, Table XXXI.

The factor coefficients are based on Bjerke's estimates,[5] which have been slightly revised to make the function homogeneous of degree one. They are 0.79 for labour and 0.21 for capital, which, incidentally, are very close to the Canadian coefficients. The resultant factor contributions are presented in Table 58.

Output in the Norwegian economy jumped from a very low rate in the earliest period to a considerably higher one in the years 1899-1930, and rose only slightly in the final period, with the latter rate very close to that of the United Sates. This

TABLE 58

SOURCES OF LONG-RUN GROWTH, NORWAY

(percentages)

	1877-1899		1899-1930		1930-1956	
Growth rate of output		1.72		2.76		2.85
Direct factor inputs:						
Labour	0.54		0.16		0.25	
Capital	0.39		0.49		0.54	
		0.93		0.65		0.80
Residual contribution °		0.79		2.12		2.05

° Inter-industry effects have not been separated from the residual.

has been the result of two disparate trends: a mild decline in total factor input resulting from the decline in labour's contribution which was not completely offset by the continued rise in capital's role; and a very sharp increase in the residual after 1899. This latter is of interest because it occurs prior to that in Canada and the United States, although they both surpass it in the latest period. An examination of the changing distribution of the labour force indicates that the gains from inter-industry shifts were lowest in the second period, invalidating that phenomenon as an explanation of the earlier growth of the residual. Some indirect evidence does suggest an explanation of this phenomenon, however. We find that the capital formation proportion in Norway rose from 13.2 per cent in the first decade of the twentieth century to 19.0 per cent in the subsequent decade.[6] In the United States, this proportion underwent a decline from 22.8 per cent to 20.9.[7] The Canadian ratio similarly fell from 24.4 to 21.1 per cent.[8] Thus the First World War led to a sharp increase, in Norway, in the share of domestic income that was devoted to investment. As much of this new investment likely incorporated many of the advanced techniques already in existence in the United States but not yet adopted by the Norwegian economy, this closing of the gap in the relative state of the arts no doubt accounts in large measure for the rapid rise in the Norwegian residual during the intermediate period. This type of discontinuity is not observed for Canada because of the continuing flow of ideas from the United States.

CHAPTER SEVEN

RECENT GROWTH EXPERIENCE, CANADA AND THE UNITED STATES[1]

DURING 1966 the performance of the Canadian economy was judged to be unsatisfactory by the nation's major advisers on economic policy.[2] Prices, which had risen moderately in 1964 and 1965, climbed at almost twice the rate in 1966. Simultaneously, the growth of output per man, a very rough measure of productivity, fell by almost one half from preceding years. These developments were judged to be potentially disastrous from the point of view of both our international competitive position and our future growth prospects.

While it is admitted that rapid price increases and declining productivity advance do have serious impacts on these crucial areas, there is room for doubt as to the seriousness of these recent developments when considered within the relevant context.

I. SECULARLY DECLINING PRODUCTIVITY IN CANADA

At the outset, we shall attempt to explain the sharp decline in the growth of output per worker in the past year. This analysis has two facets, a historical context and a comparative context.

On the historical side, one is tempted to conclude from a casual examination of the performance of the economy in the previous two years that our greatest fears are valid. Thus, in 1964, output per worker grew by 2.8 per cent, in 1965 by 3.1 per cent, but in 1966 by 1.7 per cent. But to consider output per man as a good measure of productivity change over short periods of time is inappropriate. It is well known that as an economy moves out of a recession, output can be augmented very rapidly through the use of previously under-utilized labour and idle capital. As a result, measured output per worker shows very high rates of increase immediately after an upturn begins. Similarly, as the economy approaches full utilization of its resources, increases in output can be attained only through building new capital and drawing in marginal workers. Thus, as a peak is approached, the growth of measured output per worker begins to fall quite rapidly.

That these patterns have held over the last cycle can be readily seen in the following table.

We will comment first on productivity changes and analyse the relationship to price movements later. It is evident that the above-mentioned theory respecting productivity changes has been applicable to the Canadian economy in the past decade or so. The participation rate is cyclically sensitive as a result of the entry

TABLE 59

CYCLICAL RELATIONSHIPS OF PRICES AND OUTPUT PER WORKER, CANADA, 1953–66
(percentages)

	Unemployment[a] rate	Participation[b] rate	Growth in output[c] per worker	Rate of[d] price change
1953	3.0	53.1	2.6	0.4
1954	4.6 T	52.9	−2.0	2.4
1955	4.4	52.9	5.3	0.4
1956	3.4 P	53.5	4.5	3.8
1957	4.6	54.0	−0.8	2.9
1958	7.0	53.9	1.7	1.9
1959	6.0	53.8	0.3	2.6
1960	7.0	54.2	0.9	1.5
1961	7.1 T	54.1	1.0	0.6
1962	5.9	53.9	3.9	1.5
1963	5.5	53.8	2.7	1.8
1964	4.7	54.1	2.7	2.5
1965	3.9	54.4	3.1	2.9
1966	3.6 P	55.1	1.7	4.6

SOURCES: [a] Percentage of labour force unemployed. T = trough. P = peak. DBS, *Labour Force Survey*, various issues.
[b] Percentage of population participating in the labour force. *Ibid.*
[c] GNP per employed worker. DBS, *National Accounts, Income and Expenditure*, various issues.
[d] Based on implicit price index for the GNP. *Ibid.*

of marginal workers into the labour force. Similarly, the growth of output per worker operates much as suggested, with rapid increases during the upswing (1955–6 and 1962–5) and a sharp drop as the peak is approached. The use of annual data suggests more variation in these relationships than is actually the case, since the first peak occurred *early* in 1957 and the second later in 1966, so that the observed decline was less drastic in the latter year.

If the *pattern of fluctuations* in output per worker has not dramatically changed, its *rate of growth* appears to have at least slowed in the most recent period. During the expansion of the mid-fifties, rates of increase of about 5 per cent were achieved, whereas in the sixties the average rate was about 3 per cent. This can be explained by the much greater slump from which the economy emerged in the latter case, and hence the longer and apparently slower pace of recovery. If we take comparable periods, such as 1964–6 and 1954–6, when the degree of unemployment was reduced by an almost identical amount (4.7 per cent to 3.6 per cent as compared to 4.6 per cent to 3.4 per cent), the average rates of increase in output per man were not significantly lower in the 1964–6 period (2.4 per cent versus 2.6 per cent for 1954-6).

With respect to recent performance of output per worker, one can only conclude that there is no indication of any significant deterioration in the productivity of the Canadian economy *relative* to the past. If one has any complaint, it is that the economy took so long to regain its potential level of output in the most recent period, and that as a result Canadians tolerated an unnecessarily prolonged period of unemployment and loss of output. The problem, then, was not one of productivity decline but of unemployment. The reasons for this will be analysed in our discussion of prices.

One cannot be entirely happy, however, with the use of output per worker as a measure of productivity. Output per worker depends very much on the amount of capital available for each worker. A measure of net productivity which adjusts for capital intensity is, in many ways, much more satisfactory. Even this is crude, however, since, as we have attempted to demonstrate in the preceding chapters, there are many other sources of productivity advance, such as education, and so forth. Following the earlier procedures we can estimate the various sources of growth for the period 1956–66. In addition, we can compare the results from this period with longer-run developments dating back to 1926. These are presented in Table 60.

TABLE 60

SOURCES OF GROWTH, CANADA, 1926–56 AND 1956–66
Contribution in percentage points

Source	1926–56		1956–66	
Labour	0.62		1.17	
Employment		1.22		1.98
Hours		−0.63		−0.60
Education		0.12		0.09
Age-sex composition		−0.09		−0.30
Net national capital	0.46		0.67	
Residential construction		0.03		0.05
Other construction		0.20		0.52
Machinery and equipment		0.20		0.13
Inventories		0.06		0.07
Net domestic capital		0.49		0.77
Canadian capital abroad		0.02		0.02
Foreign capital in Canada		−0.05		−0.12
Total measured inputs	1.09		1.84	
Net factor productivity	2.80		2.34	
Growth rate of output	3.89		4.18	

NOTE: The estimates for the 1926–56 period differ slightly from Table 12A because of some minor adjustments to ensure comparability.
SOURCE: A. Bowen, *Sources of Recent Economic Growth in Canada, 1956–66*, unpublished paper, Carleton University, 20.

Despite the very sharp increase in the role of capital and in labour, the growth of output has not accelerated significantly. This implies that the growth of net factor productivity has slowed down, as we see in the decrease from 2.80 per cent to 2.34 per cent in Table 60. It is crucial to explain this, as it might signal vital problems facing the Canadian economy.

In chapter 4, we examined this productivity term and found that 0.77 percentage points of the productivity term could be explained by inter-industry shifts. These are movements of factors from low-productivity industries, such as agriculture, to higher ones, raising the level of output thereby. This would leave a true productivity term of about 1.94 per cent in the period 1937–61. For the period 1956–66, we can undertake a similar calculation.

The rate of increase in output per man as a result of these shifts was about 0.34 per cent, which is less than half the longer-term rate. While the latter is strongly affected by the rapid structural readjustments after the war, there is little doubt that this process is becoming a less and less significant element in measured growth. This stems in part from the rapidly approaching limit to the relative decline in agriculture which was the major source of these gains in the past and from the fact that the net gainer has been increasingly the service industries, where the productivity margin over agriculture is much narrower than for the other industries. Further shifts into resource industries from other areas such as services are a possibility but are highly unlikely with the demands of the nation shifting from goods to services. One form of assistance to this process would be the substitution of capital for labour in low-productivity industries, but these industries seem least adaptable to the rapid technological developments of the past decade.

This decline in net factor productivity is thus due to a slowing down of the movement of resources from least- to most-productive industries. If we remove this shift effect, we discover that the rate of growth of "true" productivity within industries was 2.0 per cent in the most recent decade, almost identical to the longer-term rate. The pessimism of those alarmed at the *secular* decline in the growth of Canadian productivity does not appear to be justified.

TABLE 61

CHANGING DISTRIBUTION OF THE LABOUR FORCE, CANADA, 1956–66
(percentages of total)

Sector	1956	1966	Weights
Agriculture	13.9	7.5	0.47
Forestry, fishing, and trapping	2.5	1.4	0.86
Mines, quarrying, and oil	2.1	1.9	1.84
Manufacturing	25.7	26.1	1.38
Construction	7.4	7.3	1.73
Transportation, storage, and communication	7.8	8.3	1.28
Electric power, and gas utilities	1.2	1.2	1.05
Trade	15.8	17.8	1.29
Finance, insurance, and real estate	3.5	4.5	1.53
Services	20.2	24.1	0.80

SOURCES: DBS, *Labour Force Survey*, special tables. Weights, Table B-15.

II. DECLINING PRODUCTIVITY RELATIVE TO THE UNITED STATES

A second dimension of the concern about Canadian productivity stems from the implications for Canada's international competitiveness of a *relative* deterioration in productivity. Since the bulk of our international involvements, including trade, labour, and capital flows, are with the United States, the comparisons will be largely with that country. We propose, first, to undertake a static comparison of the two economies, initially at the aggregate level for the national economy, and then at the sectoral and industry level. Subsequently, we shall examine changes in the relative position of the two economies in the past decade to see if it has remained stable and, if not, to determine what factors are leading to the observed changes. Finally, we shall attempt to place the current situation into a longer historical perspective to assess the direction and implications of economic development for the two economies.

The tool that we shall rely on is similar to that used in preceding chapters. It might appear strange to employ such an instrument for static analysis cross-sectionally, but there is nothing in the model that precludes such an application. Indeed, the similarity in the structure of the two economies makes such an inquiry potentially very promising.[3]

It would be preferable to compare the performance of the two economies in a recent year. Unfortunately, the lack of data makes such a comparison, especially at the aggregate level, impossible. There are data for an earlier period, however, and it is instructive to undertake the analysis for that period, which we can then update, insofar as that is possible, in our next section.

We are obliged to use a period for which substantially full employment of men and capital prevailed. Otherwise, one must deal with factor and product prices that are out of equilibrium. This is not to claim that full-employment years provide true equilibrium observations, but only to suggest that these periods are closer to equilibrium situations than those where under-utilization is serious. The year we shall select is 1956, because it is the last full-employment year prior to 1966 in both economies.

The advantages of employing such a model are most readily appreciated when simple cross-sectional comparisons are attempted. Let us look at some comparisons of the kind usually made to illustrate this point. We include the comparisons for 1966 as well as for 1956 to show how the relative positions have changed (Table 62).

It can be seen that the disparity in income in the two countries depends on the concept used for the comparison. The major difference between the current dollar GNP per worker and per capita is largely due to the higher participation rate in the United States. For analysing technology, the per worker comparisons are most relevant. If we are concerned with welfare, the income per capita is more useful, and we see that there is reasonable consistency in the ratio at about 1.3:1. In other words, per capita income in the United States is about 30 per cent higher than in Canada. One slight trend is evident, and that is for the gap to widen in *all* measures—this reveals a relative deterioration in Canadian welfare over the decade, and this will warrant some careful consideration subsequently, since it strongly suggests declining relative productivity.

Since our analysis is primarily concerned with technology, we shall try to explain the differences in income on the production side. For each country, we fit the Cobb-Douglas production function and compare their components for the two countries.

To discover the source of the observed discrepancy in per worker GNP of 19 per cent in 1956, we require information on capital and factor coefficients. Net capital-stock estimates have been developed by the United States Department of Commerce,[4] and in 1956 these are estimated to be $766 billion in constant 1947-9 prices. For Canada, I have used my own estimates of net stock in 1956 in constant 1949 prices, which have been calculated to be $51.6 billion.[5]

Very great possible sources of error arise in these capital-stock estimates. We

TABLE 62
BASIC UNITED STATES/CANADA DIFFERENTIALS, 1956 AND 1966

		Canada	U.S.	Ratio U.S./Canada
Output (billions of dollars)				
GNP—current dollars	1956	30.6	419.2	13.71:1
	1966	57.8	739.5	12.80:1
GNP—current	1956	30.6	412.5	13.49:1
Canadian dollars[a]	1966	57.8	796.7	13.79:1
GNP—constant 1957 dollars	1956	31.5	434.9	13.80:1
	1966	47.4	631.5	13.31:1
Population and labour force (millions)				
Population	1956	16.1	168.9	10.51:1
	1966	19.9	196.8	9.88:1
Civilian labour force	1956	5.8	67.5	11.64:1
	1966	7.4	77.0	10.38:1
Income (dollars)				
GNP per worker—current	1956	5,289.7	6,207.6	1.17:1
dollars	1966	7,787.2	9,598.8	1.23:1
GNP per worker—constant	1956	5,431.0	6,443.0	1.19:1
1957 dollars	1966	6,405.4	8,201.3	1.28:1
GNP per capita—current	1956	1,901.9	2,481.9	1.30:1
dollars	1966	2,900.8	3,756.8	1.30:1
GNP per capita—current	1956	1,901.9	2,442.2	1.28:1
Canadian dollars[a]	1966	2,900.8	4,047.4	1.40:1
GNP per capita—constant	1956	1,959.3	2,574.8	1.31:1
1957 dollars	1966	2,381.1	3,208.2	1.45:1
Utilization adjustments[b]				
Potential GNP—constant				
1957 dollars	1956	31.6	440.1	13.91:1
(billions of dollars)	1966	47.7	637.2	13.35:1
Potential GNP per worker—				
constant 1957 dollars	1956	1,967.2	2,605.6	1.32:1
(dollars)	1966	2,396.0	3,237.1	1.35:1

NOTES: [a] Adjustment of U.S. data to Canadian dollar, by average spot rate in Bank of Canada, Statistical Summary (January 1967) 72; and 1964 Supplement, 133.
[b] Adjustment to 3 per cent unemployment rate: 1956, United States = 4.2 per cent, Canada = 3.4 per cent; 1966, United States = 3.9 per cent, Canada = 3.6 per cent.
SOURCES: Canada: DBS, National Accounts, Income and Expenditure, various issues; United States: U.S. Government Printing Office, Economic Report of the President (Washington, 1967).

have cross-checked the United States by referring to the Kendrick estimates of reproducible capital. The Canadian data can be corroborated with reference to the estimates of T. M. Brown,[6] which give $81.2 billion in 1956 in 1957 prices. Deflating by the implicit price deflater for business investment gives an estimated net stock of $56.6 billion in 1949 prices. These differences are sufficiently slight so that our findings are not significantly altered.

As for the factor coefficients, the best available estimates for the United States are those of Denison[7] ($a = 0.73$). My own for Canada, based on a similar calculating procedure, gave an $a = 0.78$.[8]

These data provide us with the tools for calculating the level of technology in the two countries.[9] For 1956, we find that Canada is marginally more productive than the United States, the difference being 0.15 per cent. If the Brown capital stock estimates are used, the United States appears to be slightly more productive by about 1.64 per cent.

The major finding of this exercise is to discover that the higher level of income per worker of 19 per cent in the United States is entirely explained by the higher level of capital per worker in the United States. Our data suggest a gap of 27 per cent in capital intensity.

The higher capital intensity of the United States is the result of a much longer period of capital accumulation in that country and reflects, in consequence, the difference in the stages of development of the two economies. Recent higher rates of capital accumulation in Canada suggest that this gap at least will begin to close. Unfortunately, the gap in income per worker has increased substantially in the past ten years, as we saw in Table 62. This implies a widening of the productivity gap. To explain this, it is necessary to attempt a production-function analysis for the United States over the past ten years and to compare it to ours for Canada, to see which sources of growth have given the United States this increased margin in productivity.

Lack of data for the total economy at present makes this quite difficult. However, the methodology can be seen in our discussion of manufacturing in the two countries in the following section.

III. PRODUCTIVITY IN MANUFACTURING

The data available for the manufacturing sectors of the two economies are much more reliable. As a result, it is useful to compare, first, the differences in *levels* of manufacturing productivity in the two economies and, second, the differing trends in this factor over the past decade.

Levels of Productivity in Manufacturing: United States and Canada

The analysis is formally identical to that in the preceding section, so we shall merely summarize the results.

TABLE 63

DIFFERENTIALS IN MANUFACTURING, CANADA AND UNITED STATES, 1956

	Canada	U.S.	Ratio U.S./Canada
Output (billions of 1957 dollars)	7.5	112.3	15.13:1
Capital (billions of 1949 dollars)	7.4	64.2	8.67:1
Labour (a) Men (millions)	1.4	17.2	12.74:1
(b) Man-hours (weekly–millions)	56.6	696.6	12.32:1
a (labour coefficient)	0.77	0.77	

SOURCES: Canada: output, DBS, *Index of Industrial Production*, various issues; labour, DBS, *Labour Force Survey* and *Employment and Hours of Work in Manufacturing*, various issues. United States: sources as given in Table 62 except for capital, which was derived from the U.S. Department of Commerce estimates contained in *The Statistical History of the United States* (Stanford, 1965), Series P 20a, Table 1, 422A and 422C, adjusted to 1949 prices.

The most striking observation is that the level of capital per worker in Canadian manufacturing is substantially higher (29 per cent) than in the United States.

This conflicts with our findings for the aggregate and would lead us to expect much higher output per manufacturing worker in Canada. Surprisingly, this is not so. The data reveal that United States manufacturing output per worker is 21.9 per cent higher. The difference is due to a very significant productivity gap between the two countries. Our analysis reveals that manufacturing productivity in the United States is 29.8 per cent higher than in Canada.

What factors might explain this differential? The foremost is, no doubt, the inefficiencies introduced into the Canadian economy and perpetuated by our tariff policy. It may be, however, that our higher capital stock per worker is an artifact, because our capital equipment is more costly than the American, so that cross-sectionally the comparison biases our stock estimates upwards. If the level of capital per worker were equal, the productivity gap would be lower, but still large at 25.6 per cent. In addition, this conclusion provides us with evidence of the cost of the tariff in forcing us to devote additional resources to real-capital formation because of our higher costs.[10]

Other factors reducing our relative efficiency in manufacturing might include the high degree of concentration in key industries. In addition, the United States invests much more heavily than Canada in research and development; and although Canada can borrow much of this new technology relatively cost-free, the technology may not be as efficient for a smaller-scale economy. Finally, the quality of the labour force in the United States is no doubt superior to Canada's, particularly as a result of its much higher levels of education, especially at the university level.[11] If we use man-hours rather than workers, the productivity gap widens further. These findings have serious implications for attempts to achieve wage and price parity in manufacturing in the two countries.

Productivity Growth in Manufacturing: Canada and the United States

Using a similar analytical tool over time, we find that up to the late fifties productivity in manufacturing grew at a slightly higher rate in Canada (2.27 per cent per year from 1937 to 1961 versus 1.96 per cent for the United States from 1929 to 1957).[12] Thus up to the end of the last decade the productivity gap would have appeared to be narrowing at a rate such that in one hundred years the differential would have been eliminated.

For our own period, 1956–66, we examined trends in manufacturing productivity to see if a significant change in these patterns was emerging. Clearly the Economic Council in its *Third Review* felt this to be the case after 1960.[13] Unfortunately, its comparison must be qualified because basic conditions in the two economies were quite different over this shorter period, as can be seen in Table 64.

It is evident that Canada reduced its severe unemployment of 1960 very much more satisfactorily over the period 1960–5 than did the United States, even though the latter started from a relatively better position in 1960. It is little wonder, therefore, that Canadian manufacturing underwent, in this artificial time span, a lower growth rate of output per worker—Canada was approaching full employment, and hence bottlenecks, much faster than was the United States.

If we compare the performance over a more meaningful period, 1956–66, we obtain the results shown in Table 65. We see that output per worker has actually

TABLE 64

UNEMPLOYMENT RATES, CANADA AND UNITED STATES, 1956–66
(per cent of the labour force)

Year	Canada	U.S.
1956	3.4	4.2
1957	4.6	4.3
1958	7.0	6.8
1959	6.0	5.5
1960	7.0	5.6
1961	7.1	6.7
1962	5.9	5.6
1963	5.5	5.7
1964	4.7	5.2
1965	3.9	4.6
1966	3.6	3.9

SOURCES: Canada, Table 59, above; United States, U.S. Government
Printing Office, *Economic Report of the President* (Washington, 1967),
Table B-20, 236.

TABLE 65

AVERAGE ANNUAL GROWTH RATE IN MANUFACTURING ACTIVITY,
CANADA AND UNITED STATES, 1956–66
(percentage)

	Canada	U.S.
Output	5.0	4.7
Labour force in manufacturing	1.5	1.0
Output per worker	3.5	3.7
Capital stocks[a]	3.5	1.6
Capital per worker	2.0	0.6

NOTE: [a] Data cover 1956–65 only.
SOURCES: Same as Table 63 above.

grown *faster* in the United States than in Canada over this decade. This has
occurred despite a significantly higher growth rate of capital per worker in
Canada. If we examine the growth rate of net factor productivity, we find that
in United States manufacturing it was 3.6 per cent,[14] far above its historical rates
noted above. For Canada, the rate of growth of productivity in manufacturing
was 3.0 per cent,[15] also above its historical rate but significantly below the recent
rate in the United States. As a result, the productivity gap which we noted for
1956 has *grown* rather than diminished by about six percentage points, raising
it to 36 per cent.

It would appear that Canada's very heavy investment in physical capital in
manufacturing has not offset the productivity gain in the United States, with the
result that output per worker has increased less rapidly here. This adds to our
concern over current discussion about wage and price parity between the two
economies, particularly at the level of manufacturing.

It is difficult to evaluate the source of this productivity differential and its
trend. The vast difference in the two countries in investing in research and
development is often noted. Consider the following information (Table 66) on
investment by the manufacturing industry in research and development in recent
years.

The fact is that United States research and development spending in manu-

TABLE 66

RESEARCH AND DEVELOPMENT EFFORT IN MANUFACTURING,
CANADA AND UNITED STATES

	Canada		U.S.
	1963	1966	1962
	(mil. $)		(bil. $)
Total R & D expenditure[a]	168	279	11.3
Business fixed investment[b]	1,347	2,803	10.9

NOTE: [a] Current and capital. [b] Plant and equipment only. Some double counting occurs because of fixed-capital formation in research and development expenditures.

SOURCES: Canada: DBS, *Daily Bulletin Supplement* (April 12, 1967), and *Private and Public Investment*, various issues. United States: U.S. Department of Commerce, Bureau of the Census, *op. cit.*, pp. 614B and 422A.

facturing is as important as fixed investment, whereas in Canada it is about one-tenth the size, and this proportion actually declined in Canada in the four years considered. Because we do not know the rate of return on research and development, we cannot include it in our model. Nevertheless, if we could assume it to be as productive as physical capital, the pure efficiency advantage of United States manufacturing would be only 14 per cent rather than between 30 and 36 per cent. Offsetting this in part is the flow of some of the benefits from United States expenditure on research and development through subsidiaries in Canada. Unfortunately, the data are so weak as to put a serious question mark over these explicit findings.[16]

In addition, and related to this, is the difference in the types of investment in the two countries. In Canada the ratio of machinery and equipment to construction-type capital has remained relatively constant at a ratio of 1:1. In the United States a much higher proportion of machinery and equipment to construction has prevailed, and this proportion has increased substantially over the decade 1956–66. Thus in 1956 the ratio was 1.5:1; it rose to 1.7:1 by 1960, and to 1.9:1 by 1966. Since it is machinery and equipment that embodies most technical advances, it may well be that the trends in research and development and in these proportions are strongly interdependent, and their joint effect might well explain the recent productivity surge in the United States.

IV. WAGE AND PRICE IMPLICATIONS

Much of the widespread concern over our productivity performance stems from alarm over the serious acceleration in prices that took place in 1966, when the *rate* of price increase exceeded that of any year since the Korean war.[17] Our criticism of concern over the performance of productivity in any one year has a direct counterpart in connection with prices. For as we reach a peak, bottlenecks begin to develop, and invariably price pressures grow. Indeed, if we adjust for the difference in dating of the peak in 1956 and 1966, the rate of price increase is not significantly different for the two booms.

If we look at price increases over a longer period, say 1956–66, we find that they averaged 2.3 per cent a year—well within the limits of acceptable price changes.

It may of course be argued that those on fixed incomes suffer even from this much inflation, but the structure of our economy makes an adjustment of their incomes an easier policy than severe price restraints. In addition, consumers began to feel the impact of inflation, but one must be careful in evaluating their reaction. The average consumer's money income increased so substantially in the past three years that even when price increases are taken into account, their real income grew at twice the average rate since the Korean war. Thus consumers as a group did indeed face severe price pressures, but these were well offset by substantial improvements in real income as a result of the economy's strong expansion. There may be certain groups of consumers that did suffer relatively more, but remedial policies are available for this problem.

The real danger of inflation in Canada is the erosion of Canada's competitive position internationally. Since Canadian trade is primarily with the United States, Canada must not permit prices to rise faster than those in the United States. As a result, it is instructive to compare Canadian price performance with that of the United States over the past decade.

Over the entire decade, Canada's position deteriorated slightly relative to that of the United States. However, one can subdivide this decade into two periods: the first, up to devaluation in May, 1962, when Canada's price performance was better than that of the United States, and the second, since devaluation, when Canadian prices have inflated at a rate some 50 per cent greater than in the United States. This latter phenomenon has in large measure been due to devaluation, particularly in the first few years. In 1962 the prices of imports rose by 4.1 per cent as compared to 1.5 per cent for all goods and services; and in 1963, by 2.9 per cent as compared to 1.8 per cent for all goods and services. By 1964 this effect had worn off, and import prices have actually grown at a very modest rate of just over one per cent since.

Two developments are primarily responsible for recent price changes. The first is the surge in food prices in 1966, which increased by 6.1 per cent and which increase was largely due to a scarcity of meat and dairy products in that year. The second is the construction boom that took place since 1963. The share of business non-residential investment in GNP increased from 13.6 per cent in 1963 to 17.3 per cent in 1966. This led to severe price pressures, particularly on construction-type investment. Prices related to construction activity showed the following rates of increase: 1963, 3.4 per cent; 1964, 4.4 per cent; 1965, 6.1 per cent: 1966, 5.3 per cent.[18]

Aggravating this source of pressure was the government construction boom associated with Expo and other Centennial activities. Measured price increases, particularly for government capital formation, substantiate this view. The performance of the government on its current-expenditure side has not alleviated these price pressures.

A final element in Canada's recent price increases relative to the United States can be attributed to more successful absorption of unemployed workers in Canada than in the United States. Had Canada maintained the same rate of unemployment as did the United States, some twenty-two thousand more workers would

TABLE 67

PRICE CHANGES[a], CANADA AND UNITED STATES, 1956-1966
(percentage)

Year	Canada	U.S.
1956	3.8	3.4
1957	2.9	3.7
1958	1.9	2.5
1959	2.6	1.6
1960	1.5	1.6
1961	0.6	1.2
1962	1.5	1.1
1963	1.8	1.3
1964	2.5	1.6
1965	2.9	1.8
1966	4.6	3.0
Average 1956-66	2.3	2.0

NOTE: [a] Implicit price deflator, GNP.
SOURCES: Canada: Table 59, above; United States: U.S. Government Printing Office, *Economic Report of the President* (Washington).

TABLE 68

CANADIAN PRICE INCREASES FOR GOVERNMENT EXPENDITURES
(percentage)

	Current	Capital	Total
1963	3.8	4.3	4.1
1964	3.6	0.3	3.2
1965	3.9	9.2	4.4
1966	6.5	8.4	6.9

SOURCE: DBS, *National Accounts, Income and Expenditure* (Ottawa, 1965 and 1966) (preliminary).

have been idle. In evaluating the cost of inflation, one must very carefully consider the alternative cost of lost income and social costs accompanying the resultant unemployment.

There is a school of thought that attributes much of our recent inflation to some cost-push mechanism operated particularly by labour. If we consider only 1966, income per worker did grow at a much higher rate than output per worker,[19] leading to a sharp rise in unit labour costs. Even over the decade 1956-66, income per worker grew slightly faster than output per worker.[20] As a result, labour's share in national income grew from 48.7 per cent to 50.8 per cent over the decade, while property's share fell from 16.7 per cent to 15.7 per cent.[21]

The real issue is whether these increases in labour income have been the cause of price increases or whether price increases have really been the result of demand pressures. This argument is particularly difficult to solve, but the Canadian situation would seem to come down in favour of the latter.

Our view is that both *aggregative* pressures on demand (including foreign, as a result of devaluation, and domestic, as a result of Expo and the boom of the mid-sixties) and *sectoral* pressures on demand (particularly from food shortages and the construction boom) combined to soak up unemployment[22] and generate substantial price pressures, particularly in the labour markets along the Montreal-Toronto axis. This has had the coincidental effect of cutting profits substantially.

The cost-push argument must imply that the demand by labour for wages in excess of labour's marginal productivity forces firms to raise prices in order to maintain profit margins. To the extent that labour has been able to do this, the argument has some validity, although it appears that other elements on the cost side must be included, such as high import prices due to devaluation, and so forth. It must also be stressed that this works only insofar as the authorities are willing to expand the money supply. Once they shut the tap, something must give; and in 1966 it was profits that did so.

What is of greater concern, however, is the failure of Canadian productivity to grow at a faster rate. If it had, the higher wages could have been maintained, along with higher profits and stable prices.

The reasons for Canada's lagging productivity, both absolutely and in terms of poor relative performance over the past decade, must therefore become our main concern. A major element is the orientation in the United States towards investing in research and development and embodying technical advances in their capital stock. In addition, the United States has cashed in on the high returns to investment in human capital. Canada's almost exclusive concern with physical capital and its reliance on imported technology do not appear to have had as high a productivity pay-off. In addition, Canada would do well to focus on the other major sources of inefficiency in its economy, including tariffs, industrial organization, and immobility of resources, all of which affect the level, and possibly the slope, of our growth path.

Another pressing question that is being raised makes the closing of this productivity gap particularly urgent. Demands for wage parity with the United States, particularly in the auto industry and airlines are now being expressed. While it is not possible to determine without a much more specialized investigation whether this is valid in the particular situation, it is clearly *not* valid for the economy as a whole. To the extent that wage bargains cannot be settled in isolation (and American research, together with our 1966 wage round, strongly suggests this to be the case), any move towards parity unjustified by a closing of the productivity gap will lead to severe inflation, to slower growth, or to higher unemployment.[23] And even if the wage round did not work, parity for some would necessarily mean an income for others far below the national average because of the aggregate productivity gap. The implications of this for our goal of equity must be carefully considered.[24]

V. CONCLUSION

Our study has revealed a large and growing productivity gap in manufacturing. This has kept incomes below those in the United States. Policies to raise them to the level of those in the United States without considering this fundamental fact of economic life must be carefully examined. At the individual firm or personal level, parity is achievable but only at the cost of distorting the economy in a variety of ways. The only way to achieve equivalent standards of living for the nation as a whole is to increase rapidly the fundamental productivity of the Canadian economy.[25]

That this is a necessary requirement for achieving income parity is strongly underlined by our findings. Canadian manufacturing accelerated its rate of productivity advance in the decade 1956–66 by 50 per cent over its historical rate. In the United States, the historical rate was almost doubled in the same period and was a full 20 per cent higher than the Canadian rate. We are therefore no longer justified in treating this factor as predetermined. Concerted effort to discover the optimal way to accelerate this process is urgently required if we are to avoid the inevitable pressures for alternative parity solutions.

CHAPTER EIGHT

SUMMARY

I. AIMS AND PROCEDURE

OUR PURPOSE in undertaking this study was to investigate recent economic growth in Canada. The technique of analysis has been patterned after Denison's monograph in which he seeks to allocate the growth of output that has occurred to the various sources that can be isolated.[1] These sources include the quantitative increase in the conventional factors of production, labour, and capital, but in addition they encompass the major changes in the quality of these factors and their contribution to economic growth. Among these latter Denison has attempted to measure and assign weights to the growing educational background of the labour force, its changing age and sex composition, the effect of declining hours of work on labour efficiency, and so forth.

In this work not all of Denison's many refinements have been followed because several of the quality adjustments were considered to be theoretically unfounded, while others, particularly those based on best guesses, were unacceptable. Those refinements that we did feel were sound were carried through for the Canadian data. In addition, we revised his findings for the United States to conform to our more limited framework, thus permitting a comparison of the experience of Canada with that of the United States.

Missing from the basic Canadian data were satisfactory estimates of capital stock. We have shown the reasons for rejecting those of the Royal Commission on Canada's Economic Prospects prepared by Hood and Scott,[2] and since no other economy-wide estimates have been published, it was necessary to build up a completely new set of estimates on both a gross and a net basis, for the total economy as well as for each of the major industries.[3]

With these new series, it was possible to pursue the analysis for the thirty years between 1926 and 1956, these terminal years being selected because of their comparability in terms of economic activity. After calculating the contributions of the quality adjusted inputs to the growth rate, we derived as a residual the growth in productivity in the two countries. To our surprise, there appeared to be a significant difference between the two sets of residuals, that of Canada being much higher than that for the United States. This was unexpected in the light of our knowledge about the technological superiority of the United States, and we felt obliged to try and explain these findings. It was decided that this could best be done at a less aggregative level of analysis, and we consequently turned to an examination of the growth of the major sectors within the Canadian economy and their counterparts in the United States.

The preliminary results of this survey indicated close similarity of residuals within comparable industries in the two countries, leaving the discrepancy in the aggregate residuals unexplained. One finding did help to resolve the problem.

With very minor exceptions, the size of each of the industry residuals were considerably smaller than the aggregate residual. The same situation held in the United States as well. Since the aggregate residual is in effect a weighted average of the industry residuals, the process of aggregation must have been picking up some element that did not really belong in the aggregate residual.

This could only be the result of changes in the industrial structure over time, and a technique for measuring these inter-industry shifts was developed. This required certain changes in the dating of Canadian experience because of data limitations, as well as the development of new series on capital stock by major industries. It was found that no serious bias was introduced as a consequence of this change.

These new measures were then employed to evaluate the effect of inter-industry shifts in the two economies, and it was found that the discrepancy between the aggregate residuals could almost entirely be explained by this phenomenon. The procedure was tested by a variety of means, such as the elimination of the service-type industries which have spurious output measures, and the estimation of the contribution of the residuals of various industries to the aggregate residual. The findings were borne out most satisfactorily by these tests.

An extension of the measurement of inter-industry effects was attempted by dis-aggregating the United States manufacturing sector into its principal industries, and considering the effect of the shifting distribution of factors of production between them. The results indicated that these shifts were important, and that taking them into account would likely serve to reconcile further the remaining disparities between the aggregate residuals of Canada and the United States.[4] In addition, further attempts at dis-aggregation, both for other major sectors and for finer industrial subdivisions, will be rewarding in adding to our knowledge about these important shifts.

The United States data permitted an additional supplement to our study. It was possible to investigate a longer period of almost seventy years and to calculate the sources of growth and the inter-industry effects in order to discover their long term trends in the growth process. A less sophisticated analysis was feasible for Canada and for a third country, Norway. Although the measurement of inter-industry shifts was not possible for these latter countries, several common elements in long-run economic growth could be discerned.

II. Findings on Long-Term Growth

In the light of this description of our procedure, we are able to summarize the findings in this work. We first consider the nature of long-run growth, so that the shorter period events can be placed in their proper historical perspective.

In all three countries we observed a continuous decline in the growth rate of man-hours of labour input. In the United States, the growth rate of man-hours fell from an early (1889-1909) level of 2.3 per cent to 0.5 per cent in the years 1929-57. In similar periods, the Canadian rate fell from 2.3 to 0.8 per cent, while the Norwegian rate fell from a much lower initial rate of 0.7 to 0.3 per cent. This decline has been due to the retardation in the growth rate of the population, reinforced by a rapidly falling number of hours worked per week. The slight increase in participation rates such as occurred in the United States has been too minute to arrest this downward trend. Furthermore, for the United States, where certain quality adjustments can be made to the man-hour series, this same sharp decline in the rate of growth of labour input can be seen even with the adjustments taken into account.

This deceleration in the growth rate of labour input appears to be a common occurrence in the growth of developed economies. From it, one can infer that the process of economic growth invariably leads to a decline in labour's role as a source of growth. The main reasons for this are likely the substitution and income effects which accompany growth. The former may arise either from the advance of productivity, which can lead to technological unemployment, or from high levels of capital accumulation such as exist in Canada and Norway, where not necessarily better, but more machinery leads to the displacement of labour. In addition, there is the tendency for the preference functions of labour to shift towards more leisure as per capita income rises in the course of development.

The sharply declining rate of growth of capital in the United States—from 4.8 per cent per annum in the earliest period to 1.0 in the latest, as opposed to its milder decline from 3.8 to 2.9 per cent in Canada and its increase in Norway from 1.9 to 2.6 per cent—is another thought-provoking finding. It can be explained by the transition of developing countries from young debtor nations, borrowing capital from abroad to finance their high rates of capital formation, to mature creditor nations, supplying these funds. With stable savings proportions, the diversion of ever-increasing funds into capital formation in foreign countries will of necessity lead to a lower rate of growth of capital in the lending country, and a more rapid rate in the borrowing country. Certainly the relationship between United States capital and Canadian growth is a convincing example of how the international flow of capital affects capital accumulation. A further explanation of the declining rate of growth of capital in the United States is that investment is occurring, but in non-material forms of capital. Rather, it is being invested in the training of man, or in the improvement of the quality of capital equipment, which improvements are understated in present measures of capital stock and its growth.

Most spectacular among the long-run findings has been the impressive growth of the residual, albeit rather grossly defined, in all three countries. In Canada, the residual contribution rose from 0.7 to 2.7 percentage points in the growth rate from the earliest to the latest period. In the United States, the residual rose from 1.1 to 2.3 percentage points over a similar period, and in Norway, the increase was from 0.8 to 2.1 percentage points. The great similarity in its magnitude and its acceleration over time leaves little doubt about the importance of this element as a source of growth in developed countries. The fact that younger countries such as Canada can achieve the same rate of advance as can the United States is of particular importance, for it offers to young developing countries the opportunity to achieve these same large gains without going through a long process of building up to current rates of technological change. Of course, this is predicated upon the existence of a proper environment for such advances.

To summarize the long-run patterns of growth, we find that in the United States the declining growth rates of labour and capital have been so great as to offset the rapid increase of the residual, with the result that the growth rate undergoes secular deceleration. For the other two economies, the decline in labour input has not been matched by a sharp fall in the rate of growth of capital, so that productivity advance has led to an acceleration in their growth rates.

An extension of this type of analysis to other countries, such as the United Kingdom and Japan, would be useful to indicate whether these findings of accelerated growth in young debtor nations and decelerated growth in older creditor nations can be generalized into a description of economic progress at various stages of development with such a description being centred on the critical role of international capital flows.

III. COMPARISONS FOR RECENT DECADES

More detailed comparisons between the growth experience of Canada and that of the United States can be made for the recent thirty-year period, particularly with reference to the quality adjustments. We find that although Canada's population grew at a much faster rate than that of the United States—1.78 per cent per annum as compared to 1.23 per cent—because of both higher rates of natural increase and greater inflows of immigrants, the participation rate declined in contrast to an increase in the United States. This, together with a reduction in weekly hours substantially greater than in the United States, led to an over-all increase of man-hours in Canada of 24.5 per cent, slightly above the increase of 17.5 per cent in the United States.

In contrast to this greater quantitative increase of labour input in Canada, the United States has reaped large benefits from the greatly improving quality of its labour force.[5] We find that in the United States the quality improvement has been almost as significant a contributor to economic growth as the physical increase in man-hours. Both education and the age and sex composition of the labour force have had greater impacts on growth in the United States than in Canada. Education has increased at twice the rate in Canada, because of a much earlier beginning in educating the majority of the population. The age and sex distribution, although of lesser importance than education in the United States, is compared to an absolute decline in its contribution to growth in Canada. This stems primarily from the restructuring of the labour force because of inter-industry shifts, particularly the decline of agriculture, but also from the effect on employment of certain institutions in that country, particularly in the field of such social welfare payments as pensions and family allowances, together with the lower earnings of females relative to their male counterparts.

The contribution of education to growth in Canada will be felt in the next two decades, and the tendency towards equal pay for women should boost the contribution of the second quality factor in the future. As a result, the current differences between the two countries should be regarded as a reflection of their relative states of development, rather than as indicative of substantial disparities in the nature of their growth.

There has been a strikingly different role played by capital in the two economies during this period. On both a gross and a net basis, aggregate capital stock in Canada has increased at a rate almost 50 per cent greater than capital in the United States. In Canada, gross stock grew at an average annual rate of 2.5 per cent, while net stock increased by 2.2 per cent. The respective growth rates for the United States are 1.9 and 1.6 per cent. This superiority holds for each of the major types of capital as well, including residential construction, machinery and equipment, business construction, and so forth.

We have investigated the sources of this growth of capital in Canada, and have found two to be of importance. First, there have been much higher savings rates in Canada over the period.[6] These have been associated with a second critical factor, and that has been the investment by the United States in the Canadian economy. In the past decade alone, for instance, foreign (chiefly American) financing as a percentage of net capital formation in Canada rose from 24 to 45 per cent.[7] Thus, as we have already stressed, one must view the rapid growth of capital in Canada as being directly connected with the slower growth of this factor in the United States.

A consideration of natural resources unfortunately led to inconclusive results because of the absence of theoretical tools needed for such an analysis. In the case of Canada, this is particularly serious, and it is hoped that further research will be directed towards incorporating this factor in models of economic growth.

Weighting the various inputs by their coefficients enabled us to determine the various factor contributions to the growth of output, and to compare these to similar contributions in the United States. As expected, quality adjusted labour input was a more important source of growth in the United States, while capital has made a greater contribution in Canada. The result is that total labour and capital contributions combined are about the same size in the two countries, accounting for approximately 1.2 percentage points in the growth rate. Since the Canadian growth rate of 3.89 per cent is much higher than that of the United States, which was 2.93 per cent, there is clearly a discrepancy in the size of the aggregate residual contributions in the two countries of significant proportions. As this aggregate residual is the most frequently used indicator of productivity advance or technological change, the reasons for this discrepancy, if discoverable, will be very useful additions to our understanding of economic growth.

We have already mentioned that the major sources of this disparity were the inter-industry shifts of the factors of production. To compute these, we devised two new measures based on assumptions of complementarity and of substitution between the factors of production. The results of applying these measures indicated that almost one-quarter of the previous aggregate residual for Canada could be ascribed to these inter-industry shifts. The tests that we developed confirmed these results.

It was felt that a similar process should be occurring in the United States, and following the aforementioned procedures, we found that only one-twentieth of the aggregate residual in that country was due to these shifts. With the aggregate residual in the United States already smaller than that in Canada—1.7 percentage points of the growth rate as compared to 2.8—the Canadian inter-industry term stands at about six times the size of the inter-industry term in the United States.

The reason for the great difference in the importance of the inter-industry effects in the two economies can be seen by examining the long-run data for the

United States. Here we find that the main element in these shifts—the shift out of agriculture—occurred much earlier and over a longer period in that country, with the main shifts taking place about the turn of the century. The result has been that inter-industry shifts have played a smaller role in that country in the recent past. For Canada, these shifts were concentrated in the thirty years under observation, 1926-56, which explains their dramatic impact.

The fact that this phenomenon is a transient element in growth suggests that one cannot expect it to play as predominant a role in the future. However, new patterns of factor shifting may come into being with either beneficial or deleterious effects on the growth of output. The latter situation could arise from major shifts out of a relatively high productivity industry, such as manufacturing, into lower productivity service industries, for example.

Since the shifts that we have accounted for referred only to broad sectoral groupings, it was decided to attempt some dis-aggregation to see if we could pick up some of the effects of intra-sectoral shifts. This was possible for manufacturing in the United States, where sixteen subsectors could be derived, and the effect of shifts between them evaluated. These were found to account for almost 10 per cent of the residual contribution of 1.8 percentage points in the manufacturing sector, and when combined with the inter-industry term of 0.11 percentage points, raised it by almost one-half to 0.15. This latter impact is due mainly to the large weight of the manufacturing residual in the aggregate residual. Shifts within manufacturing in Canada increased the inter-industry term by 0.07 percentage points to 0.73.

Removing these shifts from the aggregate residuals in the two countries produces "true" residuals that are quite close in size. In the case of the broadly defined aggregates of Table 37, the Canadian true residual is 2.3 percentage points, while that for the United States is 1.8. For the more limited aggregates, these are 2.9 and 2.6 percentage points respectively. These results were to be expected, given our findings that the residuals within similar industries in the two countries were remarkably alike, and that the distribution of inputs by industry have become almost the same so that the contribution of the industrial residuals to the aggregate residual have roughly the same weights.

These investigations suggest that the inter-industry effect has been neglected in current analyses of growth at the aggregate level. The size of its role in growth indicates how serious this oversight has been. With further analysis into shifts at more detailed levels, an accurate picture of the part played by this element in the development of Canada and the United States may emerge to broaden our understanding of economic growth.

IV. Unexplored Problems

Unfortunately, explicit incorporation of the part played by foreign trade was not possible because of the limitations of our model. The growth of Canada has been in part dependent on the foreign sector, so that such an omission is regrettable. The development of dynamic input-output models, permitting an evaluation of the impact of trade on the growth of the various industries, and thereby on total economic growth, would greatly enhance our appreciation of the role of this most critical factor.

Several other areas requiring further research should be mentioned, for the comprehension of the growth process in Canada is very much dependent on them. First there are the data problems, involving both gaps and serious weaknesses of already published material. The output data by industry should be extended back to 1926 at least, and hopefully even further into the past. In addition, much work is required to develop meaningful measures of output in the service-producing industries to remove the present downward biases of the published series. As the quality problem is particularly difficult in measuring output in all sectors of the economy, concerted efforts to incorporate this aspect of growth will be necessary.

Further understanding of the role of labour in growth will require more information about the changing quality of the labour force, including the aspects of its training other than that of formal education, such as on-the-job instruction, adult education, and the like. In conjunction with this, the development of more detailed capital stock estimates by the Dominion Bureau of Statistics should provide us with more satisfactory input measures.

Besides these gaps in data, there is room for elaboration of the model itself. Empirical and theoretical research into the size of the scale coefficients at both the industry level and for the economy as a whole is a most important task. At present, the scale effects are being concealed within the residual, giving us a false impression of the latter as well. The technique of guessing at the size of the scale factor is not enlightening.

APPENDIXES

APPENDIX A

I. Capital Stock in Canada, 1926-56

WITH THE AVAILABLE DATA, the only feasible approach for estimating capital stock is the perpetual inventory method. This necessitates a series on deflated investment going back a number of years equal to the service life of the type of capital being measured. Hence, for buildings with a service life of fifty years, an estimate of the capital stock in 1926 requires relevant investment data going as far back as 1876. Needless to say, the reliability of these data varies inversely with their age. Thus, where the data after 1926 are quite good, they are somewhat weaker in the period 1896-1926 where we have relied mainly on Buckley's investigations,[1] and prior to this where we have used Firestone's estimates[2] together with occasional primary sources.

In deriving our estimates of gross and net capital stock, we have used the methodology described by Hood and Scott,[3] although we have made use of some data that have been published subsequent to their study. Lacking sufficiently refined investment data capable of yielding an industrial distribution of capital stock as far back as 1926, we had to resort to a somewhat grosser subdivision into the following categories: residential construction, machinery and equipment, government construction, and a residual construction series which we shall call business construction.

Residential Construction

This series includes most government residential construction[4] and all other residential construction. We obtained an index of the annual increase in the housing stock from Firestone.[5] This was linked to Buckley's series on housing construction[6] distributed to an annual basis by his Table A-2 and deflated by his implicit cost of construction index.[7] This was then linked to the national accounts residential construction series to get the entire series in constant (1949) dollars. The national accounts series is obtained by summing private and government residential investment[8] and deflating this by the implicit price index of new residential construction. We estimated the service life of residential-type capital to be fifty years, following Hood and Scott,[9] to obtain our gross stock estimate for this category.

Machinery and Equipment

For the period 1926-56, we used the constant (1949) dollar investment series in PPI.[10] For earlier investment data we used Buckley's estimates for machinery and equipment distributed to an annual basis.[11] This was deflated by the price index for iron and its products[12] and then linked to the more recent series in the quinquennium 1926-30. We estimated the service life to be sixteen years by taking a weighted average of the service lives of machinery and equipment in the various sectors of the economy as given in Hood and Scott.[13]

Business Construction

With an estimated service life of fifty years, obtained by trial and error to correspond to Hood and Scott's estimates, it was necessary to obtain investment data going as far back as 1876. Firestone has made some rough calculations of this component of investment in constant (1935-9) dollars for the years 1870, 1890, and 1900.[14] For the intervening years it has been necessary to interpolate on the basis of his constant dollar GNE figures[15] adjusted for the rising trend of investment as a proportion of GNE.[16] This was then converted to 1949 prices and linked to our 1896-1926 series. The latter consists of Buckley's Table B[17] with government and residential housing investment removed, and this net item has been deflated by his implicit cost of construction index.[18] This series was then tied to the national accounts data for 1926 through 1956[19] to yield the entire investment series in prices of 1949.

Government Construction

The current treatment of government in the national accounts has required some omissions on our part in the estimation of government capital. This arises because the only income imputed to government capital in Canadian social accounting is the net rent on government buildings. Since no income directly accrues to government machinery and equipment, nor to engineering and road construction by government, we are not able to use these series in our present analysis.

With the majority of government expenditures on construction prior to 1896 being undertaken by the federal government, and these being the only construction series for government sufficiently refined, we decided to employ it as the index of government construction.[20] This current dollar series was deflated by a cost of construction index and linked to our index of real investment for 1896-1926. This is obtained from Buckley's government investment series[21] which was adjusted to remove machinery and equipment and road construction. Using his implicit cost of construction index to deflate this residual series, we linked it to Hood and Scott's government building construction[22] which we projected from 1955 to 1956.

With the gross stocks in these four sectors thus estimated, we proceeded to derive net stock data, once more following the procedure developed by Hood and Scott. The resultant series are given in the following pages.[23]

TABLE A-1

RESIDENTIAL CONSTRUCTION
(in millions of 1949 dollars)

End of year	Gross stock	Net stock
1926	9816.3	6486.0
1927	10092.4	6694.7
1928	10394.6	6918.9
1929	10673.5	7137.0
1930	10963.2	7286.5
1931	11229.5	7389.2
1932	11372.7	7364.6
1933	11483.9	7305.1
1934	11636.4	7282.4
1935	11833.0	7291.7
1936	11986.4	7343.0
1937	12268.4	7439.3
1938	12523.9	7503.9
1939	12833.2	7614.4
1940	13139.4	7720.7
1941	13534.2	7904.9
1942	13888.5	8040.2
1943	14228.0	8152.4
1944	14497.1	8286.8
1945	14936.6	8486.9
1946	15400.5	8754.2
1947	15959.9	9095.2
1948	16523.8	9441.0
1949	17234.2	9932.5
1950	17969.5	10458.8
1951	18606.3	10968.4
1952	19213.8	11362.2
1953	19938.5	11900.9
1954	20673.6	12457.1
1955	21481.9	13097.6
1956	22299.6	13793.0
1957	22981.4	14359.7
1958	23916.7	15132.5
1959	24716.1	15823.0
1960	25253.8	16274.2
1961	25784.9	16716.2

TABLE A-2
BUSINESS CONSTRUCTION (NON-RESIDENTIAL, NON-GOVERNMENT)
(in millions of 1949 dollars)

End of year	Gross stock	Net stock
1926	15998.9	10840.6
1927	16434.8	11022.6
1928	17046.8	11370.9
1929	17759.7	11809.0
1930	18300.2	12089.0
1931	18676.9	12196.0
1932	18807.3	12048.5
1933	18863.3	11822.4
1934	18933.0	11618.1
1935	19034.5	11455.4
1936	19199.9	11343.7
1937	19413.1	11276.7
1938	19596.9	11181.5
1939	19776.1	11075.6
1940	20015.7	11029.1
1941	20346.6	11084.8
1942	20750.9	11201.9
1943	21150.1	11300.0
1944	21394.5	11232.0
1945	21632.0	11156.2
1946	22076.6	11292.6
1947	22667.6	11551.2
1948	23394.8	11947.9
1949	24179.4	12400.0
1950	24997.6	12904.5
1951	25848.9	13478.6
1952	26805.4	14196.7
1953	27757.4	14966.6
1954	28642.0	15683.5
1955	29572.3	16475.7
1956	30809.3	17700.3

TABLE A-3

MACHINERY AND EQUIPMENT, EXCLUDING GOVERNMENT
(in millions of 1949 dollars)

End of year	Gross stock	Net stock
1926	4867.5	2526.4
1927	5085.4	2775.2
1928	5273.6	3093.4
1929	5521.7	3497.8
1930	5792.2	3760.7
1931	5969.5	3756.7
1932	5961.3	3577.6
1933	5891.0	3359.0
1934	5868.6	3203.8
1935	5867.9	3103.0
1936	5908.8	3059.3
1937	6066.4	3160.0
1938	6280.3	3236.8
1939	6396.3	3271.3
1940	6750.4	3509.5
1941	7258.0	3889.6
1942	7514.0	4118.0
1943	7350.0	4037.4
1944	7210.0	4074.0
1945	7094.0	4241.4
1946	7263.0	4575.0
1947	8091.0	5307.1
1948	9167.0	6071.4
1949	10331.0	6816.5
1950	11464.0	7516.8
1951	12698.0	8300.3
1952	13991.0	9122.7
1953	15236.0	9963.3
1954	16285.0	10516.1
1955	17415.0	11055.3
1956	18742.0	11931.9

TABLE A-4
GOVERNMENT CONSTRUCTION
(in millions of 1949 dollars)

End of year	Gross stock	Net stock
1926	528.5	289.5
1927	549.5	309.9
1928	561.7	321.1
1929	578.6	336.8
1930	610.4	367.0
1931	632.6	387.5
1932	644.7	395.4
1933	641.7	397.1
1934	637.2	401.1
1935	638.2	407.2
1936	646.4	411.1
1937	660.4	417.1
1938	678.4	426.7
1939	704.0	444.0
1940	862.7	596.6
1941	1161.2	881.4
1942	1524.1	1223.8
1943	1823.0	1496.8
1944	1963.4	1605.0
1945	2036.3	1642.7
1946	2064.1	1633.6
1947	2106.8	1638.4
1948	2167.7	1660.9
1949	2239.4	1693.4
1950	2324.7	1739.0
1951	2467.9	1840.8
1952	2677.6	2006.3
1953	2858.8	2139.5
1954	3017.5	2247.9
1955	3197.4	2374.9
1956	3408.4	2527.8

TABLE A-5

Hood and Scott Capital Stock Estimates, for Canada

(in millions of 1949 dollars)

Year	Sum of industry estimates		Direct cumulation	
	Net stock	Gross stock	Net stock	Gross stock
1945	8,628.6	16,595.7	7,641.1	18,119.7
1955	13,821.1	23,827.1	12,333.2	20,902.6

SOURCES: Sum industry, Hood and Scott, *Output, Labour and Capital,* Series 8000, 434 for gross and 444 for net. Direct cumulation, *ibid.,* Series 8002A, 451, Table 6B.7.

The divergence in the series, especially the trend in the gross stock figures over so short a space of time, indicates how weak the direct cumulation estimates are.

In addition to the reproducible capital goods estimated thus far, it is necessary to account for the growth in the nation's inventories and in its international assets. We estimate the value of inventories in 1926 and in 1956 as follows: Buckley estimates that in 1900, the book value of inventories in current dollars was 560 million dollars.[24] We bring this to 1926 prices by deflating this stock by the wholesale price index (1929 $=$ 100),[25] and then convert it to 1949 prices by deflating again by the implicit price index of inventory investment.[26]

With the 1900 stock of inventories now in prices of 1949, we require only the annual change in inventories in the same prices to obtain the gross stock in constant dollars for any year thereafter. Between 1900 and 1926 we have Buckley's estimates of changes in inventories[27] which we deflate first by the wholesale price index and then by the implicit index. This is linked to the national accounts series of constant (1949) dollar inventory changes[28] to give us the entire series in constant prices.

Adding these annual changes to the 1900 stock figure gives the following gross stock estimates:

TABLE A-6

Gross Stock of Inventories, Canada

(in millions of 1949 dollars)

	Gross stock
1926	6,484
1956	12,363

As for the stock of international assets, we must evaluate the Canadian holding of real assets abroad, and foreign holdings of domestic assets. The value of Canadian capital invested abroad in current prices increased from $926 million in 1926 to $4,900 million in 1956.[29] Over the same period, foreign capital invested in Canada rose from $4,569 million to $13,500 million.[30]

Deflating these figures presents some particularly difficult theoretical as well as practical problems. We shall adopt an often-used expedient and deflate both series by the implicit price deflator for Canadian GNP. The small coefficients of these components ensure that no major bias is introduced by this procedure.

Table A-7 presents the estimates of these items.

TABLE A-7

VALUE OF INTERNATIONAL ASSETS, CANADA
(in millions of 1949 dollars)

Year	Canadian investments abroad	Foreign investments in Canada
1926	1,362	6,719
1956	3,816	10,514

II. QUALITY ADJUSTMENT FOR THE CANADIAN LABOUR FORCE

TABLE A-8

THE GROWTH OF MAN-HOURS, CANADA, 1926-56

Sector	1926	1956
Agriculture:		
Employment, thousands	1,251	776
Average weekly hours	64.0	55.3
Man-hours/week, millions	80.05	42.91
Non-agriculture:		
Employment, thousands	2,299	4,826
Average weekly hours	49.8	41.3
Man-hours/week, millions	114.49	199.31
Total economy:		
Man-hours/week, millions	194.55	242.23
Implicit average weekly hours	54.8	43.2

SOURCES: Employment, DBS, *Canadian Statistical Review*, 1959 Supplement, 35, and Reference paper no. 23, *Canadian Labour-Force Estimates, 1931-1945*, 1957 revision; Hours, DBS, *Canadian Statistical Review*, 2, Table 1; Hood and Scott, *Output, Labour and Capital*, Royal Commission on Canada's Economic Prospects (Ottawa, 1957), 202, Table 55.

Changes in the age and sex composition of the Canadian labour force can be dealt with by taking the census groupings of the labour force, distributed by age and sex, and weighting each group by some measure of its average skill. This enables us to estimate the change in the average skill of the entire labour force over time. We use, as our measure of skill, the earnings of the particular groups. Thus, we assign a weight of unity to males between the ages of forty-five and fifty-four because they receive the highest average earnings. Every other age group for both men and women is given a weight equal to the proportion of its mean earnings per worker to that of the control group.

If the structure of earnings of all groups relative to the control group remained constant, one base year would suffice for obtaining a weighting scheme. However with shifts in this structure over time, it would be preferable to revise the weights in order to reflect adequately these shifts. Table A-9 indicates the change in the average quality of the labour input using both a single and a changing weighting scheme.

In both indexes we observe that the increase in the numbers of the labour force

TABLE A-9

INDEXES OF QUALITY CHANGE BASED ON AGE AND SEX, CANADA

Year		1931 weights	1931 and 1941 weights
1921		95.10	94.70
1926	(interpolated)	97.55	97.45
1931		100.00	100.00
1941		97.60	95.00
1951		97.20	93.90
1956		94.40	91.50

SOURCES: Age-sex distribution: 1921 Census, IV, 92; 1931 Census, VII, 670, Table 40; 1941 Census, VII, 516; 1951 Census, IV, Table 19; 1956 Senate Committee on Manpower and Employment, 38, Table H. Weights: 1931 Census, V, 16, Table 8; 1941 Census, VI, 70, Table 5.

surpassed the increase in adult male equivalents, causing the observed slight deterioration in the average quality of the labour force.

Part of this result may arise from our selection of only 1931 and 1941 as the base years. This was necessitated by the altered format of the 1951 census data. These years were both in periods when the economy faced major disruptions arising first from the Great Depression and then from the Second World War. We cannot, however, say that these were abnormal events and proceed to ignore them, for between them they dominated almost one-half of the period under study, and the kind of growth that was generated in these thirty years is in very significant ways determined by these events.

We shall use the single weighting scheme because the distortions that occurred during the war, causing the quality as measured by age and sex composition to deteriorate even further, were likely to have been reversed in the properous decade that followed it. The 1961 census gives us greater perspective by which to judge the validity of this assumption, and we find that there was almost no change in the index between 1956 and 1961. Thus, while the trend is not reversed, the decline appears to have halted.

In order to derive weights capable of reflecting the different productivity levels of the members of the labour force as a result of differences in the amount of formal education received, we require information relating earnings to years of schooling. There is nothing similar to the detailed United States data which permitted the analysis undertaken by Professor Houthakker.[31] Some published data do contain a distribution of income and earnings by age and sex and kind of school completed, but on a much broader basis.[32]

The implied weights in these two studies are presented in Table A-10, together with those derived from Houthakker's study but combined to fit into the grosser Canadian classification scheme.

The discrepancy between the two Canadian series is mostly due to the different coverage and perhaps also the fact that the earlier estimates were made from a small sample survey. Thus we shall employ the later estimates, based on the 1961 Census in our analysis.

With the weighting scheme thus chosen, we require a distribution of males in in the labour force by the amount of education received. No breakdown into

TABLE A-10

A COMPARISON OF US EARNINGS DIFFERENTIALS FOR
WEIGHTING CANADIAN DATA WITH CANADIAN DIFFERENTIALS

Amount of formal education	Index of mean rent-adjusted income		
	US	DBS 1959	DBS 1961
Elementary or less	100.0	100.0	100.0
Secondary	129.8	116.3	129.3
University	183.1	153.4	179.8

SOURCES: DBS 1959 from DBS, *Preliminary Statistics of Education*,
50, covers males whose major source of income is Earned income.
DBS 1961 from Podoluk, *Earnings and Education*, 21, covers male
wage and salary earners.

ages and no consideration of females is required because our earlier adjustment
accounts for differentials between these groups. The necessary data are given in
Table A-11.

TABLE A-11

DISTRIBUTION OF MALES IN CANADA, AGES 25-59,
BY AMOUNT OF FORMAL EDUCATION
(thousands of men)

Amount of formal education	1941	1951	1961
Elementary or less	1,594.9	1,668.6	1,745.8
Secondary (Grades 9-12)	774.9	847.5	1,652.3
University	191.3	299.5	333.0

SOURCES: 1941 Census, III, 659, Table 46; 1951 Census, II, Table
27; 1961 Census, I-3, Table 102.

This type of data is not available for earlier years. To estimate them for the
period prior to 1941 is particularly difficult for Canada because of the large
amount of migration; for example, in the years 1951-56, 762,000 immigrants came
to Canada and 179,400 Canadians emigrated to the United States alone.[33] As
there is no information available on the educational background of these groups[34]
one cannot make an accurate estimate of the changing quality of the domestic
labour force by cohort projections in order to cover the remote periods. Our
expedient under these circumstances has been to extrapolate the increase for
1941-51, which was 2.16 per cent over the period 1926-1941. From 1951 to 1956
we interpolate the rate of increase that occurred between 1951 and 1961, which
was 2.38 per cent. As a result, the change in the educational background of the
labour force is calculated to be 6.85 per cent between 1926 and 1956.

III. THE CALCULATION OF FACTOR COEFFICIENTS, CANADA, 1926-56

For the 1949 coefficients, we estimate that the labour share in national income
excluding military pay and allowances was 78.70 per cent.[36] We also calculate
that income payments from foreign countries to Canadians were 0.65 per cent of

national income, while payments to foreigners amounted to 3.05 per cent of national income.[36]

This leaves 23.71 per cent of net national income as the share of domestic property. The share of residential assets was estimated by data provided by DBS. The share of agriculture in property income was estimated from the income of farm operators with the labour component removed.[37] The remainder was then obtained as a residual.

Agricultural assets were divided into land and capital according to their value in 1941.[38] Capital was then divided into inventories, construction, and machinery and equipment by using the value of each in 1949.[39] Residential assets were similarly distributed,[40] as were the remaining assets.

For the 1926-56 coefficients, the same procedure was used for labour, and for international income payments. However, the property component could not be subdivided for lack of data, and only the total property share could be used in conjunction with the growth of all capital taken as a whole.

THE SHORTAGE OF CAPITAL STOCK SERIES necessitated our estimation of gross and net capital stock over the period 1937-61. We have made use of Hood and Scott's estimates of average service lives of the two types of capital—machinery and equipment, and construction-type—for the ten sectors. For the years after 1926, satisfactory information on current dollar investment is published in the Department of Trade and Commerce's *Public and Private Investment in Canada, 1926-1951*, its revision in 1959 covering the years 1946-57, and the DBS publication *Outlook*, which retains the same classification. We shall hereafter refer to these sources as PPI. The lack of good price indexes led us to decide upon the use of the more general implicit price deflators for machinery and equipment and for non-residential construction, which are published in the national accounts, Table 6. Since these have 1949 as their base, their use complements the rest of our study, which takes 1949 as the base year. We now turn to a detailed discussion of the derivation of our capital stock estimates for each industry.

Agriculture

(a) Construction (service life of forty years). Investment data prior to 1926 are obtained from Buckley's Table VIII page 22. As these are given for quinquennia only, we distributed them to an annual basis by his Table C class 1. As a deflator for this series we used Buckley's Implicit Cost of Construction index in Table A-2. Since this gives us a constant dollar series in 1913 dollars, it was necessary to translate it into 1949 dollars by linking it to the figure for 1926 in prices of 1949. The investment data after 1926 are obtained from PPI, which we deflated by a specially constructed price index combining a wage rate index for the construction industry with a price index of farm building materials in the proportions indicated by Buckley (88).

(b) Machinery and equipment (service life of thirteen years). Investment data for 1921-5 are from Buckley's D class 1 distributed to an annual basis by Table C class 1 and linked with PPI in 1926. The entire series is deflated by the price index of farm machinery as given in the DBS bulletin *Prices and Price Indexes*, after the latter was converted to a 1949 base.

Forestry, Fishing, and Trapping

(a) Construction (service life of twenty-one years). Only forestry is included in this series. Investment in constant dollars for the years 1916-25 was obtained from an index of physical production of pulpwood and lumber products in the *Canada Year Book, 1929*. This series was linked to the figure for 1926 in constant

(1949) dollars. Investment data after 1926, obtained from PPI, were deflated by the Implicit Price Deflator for non-residential construction, given in the national accounts.

(b) Machinery and equipment. For forestry, the estimated service life is nine years. We deflated PPI data for forestry by the implicit price deflator for machinery and equipment in the *National Accounts*. For fishing, the service life is six years. After 1955, it was necessary to separate fishing from the published total of "Agriculture and Fishing" by taking 6.28 per cent of this total. The same deflator as for forestry was employed.

Mining, Quarrying, and Oil Wells

(a) Construction (service life of twenty-five years). Investment for 1911-25 was estimated using an index of investment in mining machinery and equipment deflated by Buckley's Implicit Cost of Construction index. This series was then put into 1949 dollars by linking the 1925 figure to that for 1926 using the index of mineral production in DBS, *Index of the Physical Volume of Business*. Investment data after 1926 were deflated by the implicit price deflator for non-residential construction.

(b) Machinery and equipment (service life of sixteen years). For 1921-5, we used Buckley's Table D classes 2, 3, and 4 distributed to an annual basis by corresponding classes in Table C. This was then deflated by the price index of iron and its products which is given in *Prices and Price Indexes* of DBS and the deflated series was linked to the 1926 figure in 1949 dollars by the same index of mineral production as above. After 1926, the investment data are deflated by the implicit price deflator for machinery and equipment.

Manufacturing

(a) Construction (service life of forty years). We used our "Business" investment series (described in chap. 1, 25) as an index of manufacturing investment for the years 1898-1925, this series then being linked to the 1926 figure in constant (1949) dollars. The investment series after 1926 was deflated by the implicit price deflator for non-residential construction.

(b) Machinery and equipment (service life of eighteen years). For investment from 1919 to 1925, we used Buckley's Table D classes 2, 3, and 4, distributed to an annual basis by corresponding classes in Table C. This is deflated by the price index of iron and its products and is then translated into 1949 dollars by linking its average for 1926-30 to that of the following series. These are PPI data deflated by the implicit price deflator for machinery and equipment.

Construction

(a) Construction (service life of twenty-five years). For 1913-25, we used the "Business" investment index as we did for manufacturing. This was linked to 1926 in prices of 1949. For the years after 1926, we deflated PPI data by the implicit price deflator for the non-residential sectors.

(b) Machinery and equipment (service life of nine years). We deflated PPI data by the implicit price deflator for machinery and equipment.

Electric Power and Gas Utilities

(a) Construction (service life of fifty-five years). For 1883 to 1925 we based our investment series on an index of the increase in hydraulic turbine horsepower installed in central electric stations and linked this to the 1926 value in 1949 dollars. Post-1926 data were deflated by the implicit price deflator for non-residential construction.

(b) Machinery and equipment (service life of thirty years). Buckley's Table D classes 2, 3, and 4 were distributed to an annual basis by similar classes in Table C and then deflated by the price index of iron and its products to give investment figures for 1908-25. This was linked to the 1926-30 average of investment in 1949 dollars. PPI data between 1926 and 1961 were deflated by the implicit price deflator for machinery and equipment.

Trade

(a) Construction (service life of fifty years). For the years 1888-1925, we used an index of "residual construction" which is derived by removing from "Business" construction the following components: construction-type investment in transportation, storage, and communication, in pulp and paper, in agriculture, in mining, and in electric power and gas. This residual series was linked to the 1926 figure in 1949 dollars. Investment after 1926 from PPI was deflated by the implicit price deflator for non-residential construction.

(b) Machinery and equipment (service life of sixteen years). For 1921-5 we took Buckley's Table D classes 8-11 and distributed them annually by corresponding classes in Table C. This was deflated by the price index of iron and its products and linked to the 1926 constant dollar figure by the index of construction-type investment. PPI data for 1926-61 are deflated by the implicit price deflator of the national accounts for machinery and equipment.

Finance, Insurance, and Real Estate

(a) Construction (service life of fifty years). This series consists of two sub-series. The first is the non-residential component and is constructed by linking the "residual construction" index to the 1949 dollar figure for 1926, and by deflating non-residential construction as given in PPI by the implicit price deflator for the years 1926-61. The second is residential construction, the derivation of which is fully described in Appendix A.

(b) Machinery and equipment (service life of fifteen years). For 1921-5, we distributed classes 8-11 in Buckley's Table D to an annual basis by Table C and deflated this series by the price index of iron and its products. This was then linked to the 1926 value in 1949 dollars. PPI data were deflated by the implicit price deflator for machinery and equipment to give investment data for 1926 on.

Transportation, Storage, and Communication

(*a*) Construction (service life of fifty years). For 1888-95, we used an index of the increase in railway mileage[1] which we linked to the 1896 figure in 1949 dollars. An index of transportation construction was developed for the period 1896-1925 using Buckley's Table J to obtain net railroad investment and replacement, the latter being separated from repair investment by using the proportions presented in Buckley (p. 118). This was deflated by his Implicit Cost of Construction index and then linked to the 1926 figure in constant dollars. Investment data after 1926 were deflated by the implicit price deflator for non-residential construction.

(*b*) Machinery and equipment (service life of sixteen years). Investment between 1921-5 was estimated by taking Buckley's Table D classes 5 and 6, distributing them annually by Table C using similar classes, and deflating this series by the price index of iron and its products. The link whereby this series was brought into 1949 dollars was made in the period 1926-30. For investment after 1926, we deflated PPI data by the implicit price deflator for machinery and equipment.

Commercial and Community Services

(*a*) Construction (service life of fifty years). The index of "residual construction" was used to obtain investment trends for the years 1888-1925. It was linked to the 1926 estimate in 1949 prices, and PPI data were deflated by the implicit price deflator for non-residential construction to complete the investment series.

(*b*) Machinery and equipment (service life of thirteen years). We distributed Buckley's classes 8-11 of Table D to an annual basis by Table C, and deflated this by the price index for iron and its products to get investment estimates for 1921-5. These were then converted into 1949 dollars by linking the 1926-30 average to that of the following series. This is PPI investment for this sector deflated by the implicit price for machinery and equipment as given in the *National Accounts*.

TABLE B-1

AGRICULTURE
(in millions of 1949 dollars)

End of year	Construction		Machinery and equipment	
	Gross stock	Net stock	Gross stock	Net stock
1937	1085.1	484.0	1172.2	552.0
1938	1070.9	474.1	1220.0	564.2
1939	1060.5	467.7	1204.0	566.6
1940	1050.3	462.7	1183.7	597.6
1941	1039.5	461.7	1123.5	634.8
1942	1020.0	458.8	1059.6	647.3
1943	1000.0	456.4	995.3	619.0
1944	990.8	462.1	1048.5	640.2
1945	993.3	473.5	1133.4	683.9
1946	998.8	499.7	1282.9	772.8
1947	1009.7	528.6	1500.0	942.3
1948	1030.3	563.8	1749.4	1133.3
1949	1044.4	612.0	2028.8	1349.7
1950	1049.2	656.0	2389.8	1657.0
1951	1096.8	699.2	2637.1	1822.9
1952	1142.8	743.6	2898.0	1977.2
1953	1191.6	787.9	3126.7	2106.6
1954	1243.4	826.6	3230.1	2097.7
1955	1301.4	859.8	3384.1	2102.2
1956	1342.5	896.7	3606.5	2117.5
1957	1366.5	926.4	3735.8	2067.1
1958	1400.9	959.9	3839.6	2007.8
1959	1441.4	995.8	3920.3	1969.2
1960	1480.5	1027.8	3910.6	1926.1
1961	1539.7	1059.2	3838.7	1859.8

TABLE B-2
FORESTRY
(in millions of 1949 dollars)

End of year	Construction		Machinery and equipment	
	Gross stock	Net stock	Gross stock	Net stock
1937	84.6	42.4	32.1	16.6
1938	84.2	42.2	30.2	16.8
1939	84.2	42.4	29.2	17.6
1940	85.2	43.6	30.8	19.4
1941	83.2	42.2	36.8	21.0
1942	84.3	42.8	40.4	22.7
1943	84.8	43.0	41.7	22.3
1944	92.5	50.9	45.5	24.4
1945	96.4	55.1	49.8	27.2
1946	99.3	58.3	54.8	31.0
1947	111.9	71.2	71.3	45.2
1948	121.5	80.5	82.0	52.2
1949	132.3	90.7	87.0	53.1
1950	143.2	100.5	95.1	59.5
1951	157.0	112.3	119.4	79.0
1952	168.8	119.8	131.9	82.3
1953	181.1	126.2	137.4	79.8
1954	198.6	137.4	145.5	80.5
1955	222.5	154.5	157.4	85.5
1956	248.3	172.7	163.0	93.9
1957	263.8	180.0	162.2	89.9
1958	272.3	180.1	161.8	81.5
1959	282.2	180.8	163.9	81.7
1960	295.2	184.6	151.7	81.4
1961	306.5	187.0	150.1	79.5

TABLE B-3

Fishing and Trapping
(in millions of 1949 dollars)

End of year	Machinery and equipment only	
	Gross stock	Net stock
1937	55.3	32.9
1938	56.7	31.9
1939	54.2	29.9
1940	52.1	29.3
1941	52.3	29.9
1942	51.3	30.7
1943	52.4	31.7
1944	57.2	36.0
1945	66.6	43.3
1946	76.7	50.7
1947	89.0	59.5
1948	100.8	66.0
1949	109.2	67.2
1950	119.7	72.5
1951	128.2	77.8
1952	134.7	81.4
1953	132.1	78.0
1954	127.1	72.3
1955	125.8	67.8
1956	120.3	64.8
1957	109.2	59.0
1958	99.9	56.5
1959	99.1	58.1
1960	101.2	60.0
1961	101.4	60.0

TABLE B-4
MINING, QUARRYING, AND OIL WELLS
(in millions of 1949 dollars)

End of year	Construction		Machinery and equipment	
	Gross stock	Net stock	Gross stock	Net stock
1937	473.2	298.0	241.6	134.9
1938	492.7	312.7	256.3	143.3
1939	511.0	321.7	270.1	151.2
1940	524.7	324.0	283.7	158.6
1941	535.0	326.5	296.4	165.5
1942	535.7	319.2	299.3	163.6
1943	535.7	309.1	292.5	154.7
1944	538.0	299.8	282.9	147.2
1945	539.7	291.8	257.4	137.4
1946	545.0	287.2	251.0	139.9
1947	562.8	292.4	262.2	146.9
1948	600.4	318.9	279.4	155.0
1949	645.7	351.9	312.2	176.5
1950	697.7	390.6	344.2	200.5
1951	768.7	448.1	384.9	213.7
1952	859.8	522.3	427.2	249.2
1953	949.9	611.0	475.9	296.4
1954	1048.4	713.0	527.6	341.9
1955	1180.4	854.3	572.8	378.0
1956	1417.6	1072.2	669.7	463.4
1957	1688.7	1292.6	785.7	562.1
1958	1840.7	1387.3	837.8	581.7
1959	1999.5	1482.4	890.1	591.4
1960	2154.3	1603.1	943.5	600.0
1961	2350.1	1751.7	987.7	593.1

TABLE B-5
MANUFACTURING
(in millions of 1949 dollars)

End of year	Construction		Machinery and equipment	
	Gross stock	Net stock	Gross stock	Net stock
1937	4283.3	2211.4	3350.2	1634.4
1938	4332.0	2181.5	3333.7	1565.4
1939	4358.8	2131.4	3287.2	1489.4
1940	4438.5	2141.5	3431.5	1588.3
1941	4538.2	2181.9	3637.2	1760.2
1942	4676.2	2271.5	3813.7	1900.9
1943	4713.7	2273.8	3834.1	1894.3
1944	4708.8	2241.0	3760.2	1878.8
1945	4713.5	2228.9	3705.3	1944.4
1946	4751.6	2283.6	3631.9	2010.8
1947	4840.0	2381.7	3636.4	2218.3
1948	4923.9	2449.2	3703.7	2433.3
1949	4936.6	2483.1	3873.7	2606.5
1950	4907.8	2487.7	4107.3	2738.5
1951	4942.5	2591.7	4502.7	2949.3
1952	5005.4	2739.4	4967.2	3219.8
1953	5072.3	2861.3	5407.0	3466.5
1954	5147.0	2953.7	5797.3	3638.3
1955	5299.4	3079.8	6142.2	3788.7
1956	5550.6	3289.5	6694.7	4117.1
1957	5783.5	3504.7	7263.2	4422.9
1958	5922.3	3626.9	7460.7	4498.4
1959	6048.0	3722.0	7617.8	4603.5
1960	6103.7	3783.6	7833.3	4738.6
1961	6181.8	3800.6	8120.2	4795.6

TABLE B-6
CONSTRUCTION
(in millions of 1949 dollars)

End of year	Construction		Machinery and equipment	
	Gross stock	Net stock	Gross stock	Net stock
1937	93.4	42.0	155.5	61.4
1938	89.1	40.5	122.2	57.4
1939	86.5	39.5	96.2	59.4
1940	85.7	38.6	96.0	64.9
1941	86.1	38.9	110.4	74.7
1942	86.8	40.5	137.1	91.8
1943	86.7	42.0	158.7	101.9
1944	86.1	43.0	169.6	105.9
1945	86.3	45.4	194.1	122.4
1946	89.5	48.4	214.4	138.0
1947	89.6	48.3	259.6	172.7
1948	94.1	53.0	298.3	198.2
1949	101.9	61.2	325.1	208.1
1950	111.3	70.4	358.5	225.9
1951	113.8	71.8	378.4	235.4
1952	114.2	71.1	409.4	249.7
1953	116.1	74.1	453.5	270.1
1954	115.7	76.3	488.6	290.1
1955	121.1	83.5	575.4	359.8
1956	129.6	89.9	653.1	431.9
1957	139.4	95.6	699.2	459.7
1958	149.7	100.7	753.1	478.9
1959	159.5	105.1	786.2	482.2
1960	166.5	107.6	813.7	471.6
1961	173.6	109.8	834.2	458.0

TABLE B-7

Electric Power and Gas Utilities

(in millions of 1949 dollars)

End of year	Construction		Machinery and equipment	
	Gross stock	Net stock	Gross stock	Net stock
1937	1511.6	1091.1	624.6	365.0
1938	1547.3	1099.3	639.0	368.8
1939	1578.5	1104.5	647.8	368.0
1940	1611.3	1110.7	652.5	366.7
1941	1673.0	1145.5	664.6	375.9
1942	1745.3	1189.5	678.0	390.8
1943	1776.7	1191.3	671.5	384.8
1944	1790.6	1175.0	665.5	373.3
1945	1825.2	1179.1	659.1	357.8
1946	1897.6	1220.4	659.6	350.9
1947	1991.6	1282.0	695.7	377.2
1948	2161.3	1417.6	758.2	427.5
1949	2387.3	1606.4	847.4	504.3
1950	2630.9	1808.7	948.9	593.3
1951	2895.1	2027.2	1055.3	686.3
1952	3206.9	2288.5	1179.8	791.7
1953	3474.3	2499.7	1311.9	902.9
1954	3701.7	2666.0	1419.4	986.2
1955	3937.5	2838.7	1505.5	1046.7
1956	4268.0	3112.1	1626.3	1145.4
1957	4687.0	3459.7	1766.0	1266.8
1958	5063.1	3756.8	1852.1	1337.9
1959	5352.6	3966.6	1941.4	1410.6
1960	5605.9	4141.2	2006.1	1456.9
1961	5865.9	4332.4	2060.8	1476.5

TABLE B-8

TRADE
(in millions of 1949 dollars)

End of year	Construction		Machinery and equipment	
	Gross stock	Net stock	Gross stock	Net stock
1937	1380.3	882.3	307.7	152.1
1938	1407.4	889.0	314.3	157.0
1939	1432.5	893.0	321.1	157.4
1940	1455.8	894.9	330.0	163.7
1941	1473.8	891.7	332.3	165.1
1942	1494.3	890.2	336.8	165.6
1943	1498.2	871.3	323.3	152.1
1944	1516.8	866.8	312.1	157.5
1945	1540.1	867.0	289.3	165.0
1946	1593.7	897.6	316.3	194.7
1947	1669.0	945.4	361.4	235.8
1948	1765.5	1011.0	421.9	284.6
1949	1861.9	1078.7	506.2	348.2
1950	1967.0	1157.1	600.7	422.6
1951	2044.9	1210.0	695.5	489.6
1952	2097.2	1244.0	766.6	529.7
1953	2214.5	1347.2	860.7	594.6
1954	2335.6	1458.2	967.8	672.0
1955	2430.3	1545.2	1064.0	727.7
1956	2502.2	1620.7	1147.0	770.6
1957	2601.5	1710.3	1241.6	815.5
1958	2710.1	1789.0	1331.0	848.6
1959	2771.5	1843.4	1455.8	897.7
1960	2827.4	1892.8	1573.3	949.7
1961	2849.5	1929.3	1664.8	969.9

TABLE B-9

FINANCE, INSURANCE, AND REAL ESTATE [*]

(in millions of 1949 dollars)

End of year	Construction		Machinery and equipment	
	Gross stock	Net stock	Gross stock	Net stock
1937	555.6	348.6	49.2	23.4
1938	559.7	345.3	49.2	22.3
1939	568.8	344.6	48.7	21.5
1940	576.7	341.8	48.1	21.0
1941	583.7	337.8	47.6	20.1
1942	588.1	331.7	43.7	18.4
1943	590.1	323.6	39.3	16.4
1944	594.1	317.3	33.8	15.8
1945	601.8	316.1	32.1	17.0
1946	612.5	318.5	33.8	20.2
1947	629.7	325.1	37.1	23.9
1948	656.8	339.6	42.9	28.8
1949	678.4	350.5	49.4	33.9
1950	721.1	383.3	59.3	42.0
1951	759.5	412.9	71.9	52.3
1952	778.2	426.1	81.5	59.1
1953	813.4	458.4	91.5	65.9
1954	869.0	510.6	102.6	73.4
1955	915.8	553.8	115.6	82.3
1956	965.5	604.9	131.8	93.1
1957	1028.6	660.5	148.7	102.7
1958	1125.5	740.4	168.4	113.4
1959	1256.5	864.2	194.7	130.5
1960	1396.3	993.5	215.0	141.3
1961	1539.6	1133.3	237.0	154.3

[*] Excludes residential construction.

TABLE B-10

TRANSPORTATION, STORAGE, AND COMMUNICATIONS

(in millions of 1949 dollars)

End of year	Construction		Machinery and equipment	
	Gross stock	Net stock	Gross stock	Net stock
1937	7585.7	4087.3	1303.1	691.7
1938	7619.4	3993.9	1367.1	719.5
1939	7626.6	3903.5	1379.7	723.8
1940	7626.3	3816.8	1406.7	727.3
1941	7617.2	3733.0	1431.3	716.8
1942	7632.5	3661.2	1451.0	724.0
1943	7691.5	3626.6	1566.6	857.7
1944	7692.7	3527.9	1794.3	1087.0
1945	7722.2	3439.2	1763.5	1129.6
1946	7788.6	3384.1	1757.1	1161.0
1947	7845.0	3336.2	1884.3	1284.5
1948	7878.2	3301.3	2074.7	1395.3
1949	7962.8	3291.6	2251.9	1476.5
1950	8056.9	3300.8	2399.7	1523.2
1951	8127.5	3293.8	2598.3	1618.2
1952	8284.2	3370.2	2799.0	1723.3
1953	8428.8	3460.9	2989.0	1854.1
1954	8524.8	3527.1	3196.0	1983.5
1955	8591.4	3595.9	3380.7	2058.1
1956	8804.4	3840.6	3641.8	2197.6
1957	9074.3	4243.4	3977.5	2383.1
1958	9307.9	4621.3	4264.9	2518.6
1959	9423.5	4860.1	4394.6	2606.1
1960	9458.7	5082.0	4418.6	2682.6
1961	9470.3	5294.6	4545.9	2688.4

TABLE B-11

SERVICES *

(in millions of 1949 dollars)

End of year	Construction		Machinery and equipment	
	Gross stock	Net stock	Gross stock	Net stock
1937	3759.5	2142.4	312.4	149.2
1938	3783.6	2117.2	305.2	146.8
1939	3836.6	2104.4	310.6	153.2
1940	3864.5	2060.8	300.0	148.5
1941	3903.0	2025.8	312.1	173.0
1942	3926.0	1978.9	296.0	172.5
1943	3944.6	1930.7	277.0	164.5
1944	3972.9	1890.8	273.6	163.9
1945	4020.9	1880.4	302.0	183.8
1946	4104.7	1909.8	330.8	201.8
1947	4217.7	1952.0	374.5	232.5
1948	4388.5	2038.4	435.3	278.2
1949	4558.9	2137.6	486.0	320.7
1950	4744.2	2257.8	552.2	372.2
1951	4917.6	2376.1	612.5	411.6
1952	5070.8	2499.3	666.2	448.1
1953	5207.9	2625.1	746.0	495.9
1954	5361.5	2766.0	796.8	536.9
1955	5559.3	2954.2	881.6	583.9
1956	5707.5	3130.5	980.6	629.9
1957	5947.1	3339.6	1075.1	669.7
1958	6261.8	3561.2	1154.5	707.3
1959	6510.9	3793.0	1241.5	746.7
1960	6762.2	4017.3	1337.7	803.5
1961	6962.0	4254.3	1424.0	861.4

* Excluding public administration and defence.

II.   RECONCILIATION OF CAPITAL STOCK ESTIMATES, CANADA

It is necessary to examine the results of our estimates in the light of extant data. As the sole published data are those of Hood and Scott, they provide the only basis for comparison. Table B-12 gives necessary information for such a test.

TABLE B-12

A COMPARISON OF NET CAPITAL STOCK ESTIMATES BY TYPE, CANADA

(in millions of 1949 dollars)

Type	Hood and Scott		New estimates	
	1945	1955	1945	1955
Residential construction	8,757	12,891	8,487	13,098
Business construction	9,824	16,161	11,156	16,478
Machinery and equipment	4,327	10,946	4,241	11,055
Government buildings	1,692	2,395	1,643	2,375
Total stock	24,600	42,393	25,527	43,004

The similarity of the results derives in large part from our following their basic procedures. Since no other information has been published for the years prior to 1945 and after 1955, it is impossible to check our data in those periods. One test of these aggregates can be made, however, by combining our sectoral totals and comparing this aggregate to business construction and machinery and equipment in comparable years. We do so for the longest possible period, 1937-56. The results are given in Table B-13.

TABLE B-13

A COMPARISON OF NEW ESTIMATES OF NET STOCK
(in millions of 1949 dollars)

Type	1937	1949	1956
Total construction *	1,277	12,400	17,700
Aggregate construction †	1,630	12,064	17,830
Total machinery and equipment	3,160	6,816	11,932
Aggregate machinery and equipment	3,814	7,145	12,125

* Total business construction. Table A-2.
† Sum of net stock, Tables B-1 to B-11.

The similarity of the aggregated figures derived from our industrial data to the totals which were obtained quite independently is due in large part to the consistency of the basic investment data in *Public and Private Investment*. Since these data begin in 1926, however, much of the earlier estimates depend only marginally on them. Thus, the greatest divergence is in the earliest year, 1937. Fortunately, the disparity is not too large, especially when contrasted to the rather greater dissimilarity we noted in Hood and Scott's parallel series.[2]

III. CONTRIBUTION OF INTER-INDUSTRY SHIFTS, CANADA, 1939-61

TABLE B-14

DISTRIBUTION OF OUTPUT BY INDUSTRY IN 1949, CANADA

Industry	GDP		NDP
	mill. $	%	mill. $
Agriculture	1601	11.371	1418
Forestry	397	2.810	361
Mining	665	3.444	566
Manufacturing	4034	29.015	3702
Construction	1090	6.770	1043
Electric power	277	1.747	218
Trade *	2109	15.454	1923
Finance	1183	9.686	795
Transportation	1244	8.875	1134
Services	1583	10.827	1464

NOTE: Trade data are given together with transportation and storage in the inter-industry study. We have allocated them on the basis of the proportions given in *National Accounts 1926-1956*, 28-9.

SOURCE: *The Supplement to the Inter-Industry Flow of Goods and Services, Canada, 1949*, Table 1, line 52 for GDP and less line 51 for NDP.

TABLE B-15

Net Earnings of Labour and Property, Canada, 1949

Industry	Estimated labour share	Net labour income	Net property income	Average income Labour °	Propertie †
	%	mill. $	mill. $	$	%
Agriculture	78.8	1117.4	300.6	0.470	15.323
Forestry	78.5	283.4	77.6	0.856	36.777
Mining	59.0	333.9	232.1	1.835	43.925
Manufacturing	73.7	2876.4	825.6	1.381	16.221
Construction	94.1	981.5	61.5	1.726	22.837
Electric power	39.9	87.0	131.0	1.052	6.206
Trade	77.3	1486.5	436.5	1.288	30.591
Finance	41.2	327.5	467.5	1.533	4.531
Transportation	77.3	876.6	257.4	1.284	5.398
Services	89.8	1314.7	149.3	0.805	6.073
	(1)	(2)	(3)	(4)	(5)

° Dollars per standardized man-hour.
† Dollars per dollar of capital.

SOURCES: (1), *Inter-industry Study*, Table 1, Row 48/49; (2) and (3), NDP of Table B-14 times (1) and NDP minus (2); (4) and (5), (2) over Table B-16 (2) in man-hours; and (3) over Table B-16 (5).

TABLE B-16

Factor Inputs, Canada, 1937, 1949, and 1961

Industry	Labour input			Capital input		
	1937	1949	1961	1937	1949	1961
Agriculture	3220.6	2377.8	1482.4	1036.0	1961.7	2919.0
Forestry	329.5	331.0	233.8	91.9	211.0	326.5
Mining	187.1	182.0	211.2	432.9	528.4	2344.8
Manufacturing	1321.8	2082.4	2221.0	3845.8	5089.6	8596.2
Construction	320.6	568.8	698.0	103.4	269.3	567.8
Electric power	46.6	82.7	110.6	1456.1	2110.7	5808.9
Trade	768.9	1154.4	1562.6	1034.4	1426.9	2899.2
Finance	147.1	213.7	346.3	7811.3	10316.9	18013.8
Transportation	462.4	682.5	713.3	4779.0	4768.1	7983.0
Services	974.8	1632.6	2399.0	2291.6	2458.3	5115.7
	(1)	(2)	(3)	(4)	(5)	(6)

SOURCES: (1) – (3), given in man-hours standardized for education, age, and sex, in millions (See Table B-17, below, for sources); (4) – (6), given in millions of 1949 dollars, from Tables B-1 to B-11.

TABLE B-17

TOTAL FACTOR INPUT IN LABOUR EQUIVALENTS
CANADA, 1937, 1949, AND 1961

Industry	Weights for capital	Capital input in Labour Equivalents			Total factor input in labour equivalents		
		1937	1949	1961	1937	1949	1961
Agriculture	0.326	337.7	639.5	951.6	3558.3	3017.3	2434.0
Forestry	0.430	39.5	90.7	140.4	369.0	421.7	374.2
Mining	0.239	103.5	126.3	560.4	290.6	308.3	771.6
Manufacturing	0.117	450.0	595.5	1005.8	1771.8	2677.9	33226.8
Construction	0.132	13.6	35.5	74.9	334.2	604.3	772.9
Electric power	0.059	85.9	124.5	342.7	132.5	207.2	453.3
Trade	0.238	246.2	339.6	690.0	1015.1	1494.0	2252.6
Finance	0.030	234.3	309.5	540.4	381.4	523.2	886.7
Transportation	0.042	200.7	200.3	335.3	663.1	882.8	1048.6
Services	0.075	171.9	184.4	383.7	1146.7	1817.0	2782.7
	(1)	(2)	(3)	(4)	(5)	(6)	(7)

SOURCES: (1), Table B-14 (5) ÷ (4), gives the man-hour equivalent of a dollar of capital in each industry; (2) – (4), Table B-16, (4) – (6) times (1); (5) – (7), Table B-16, (1) – (3) plus (2) – (4).

IV. LABOUR INPUT ADJUSTED FOR QUALITY BY INDUSTRY, CANADA

TABLE B-18

COMPONENTS OF LABOUR INPUT INDEX
(Level of indexes in 1961 with 1937 = 100)

Industry *	Labour	Man-hours	Education	Age-sex	Adjusted	Growth rate
						%
Agriculture	51.61	44.05	102.37	104.65	47.62	−1.77
Forestry	76.00	70.38	102.54	98.34	70.97	−1.07
Mining	132.84	109.09	104.52	99.05	112.94	0.51
Manufacturing	193.02	164.63	102.73	100.89	170.94	2.25
Construction	232.70	220.60	103.05	95.77	217.71	3.30
Electric power	278.89	238.03	104.40	96.68	240.24	3.72
Trade	231.60	195.35	104.50	98.91	201.93	2.97
Finance	249.01	230.41	107.96	94.82	235.87	3.64
Transportation	180.39	153.73	103.64	96.80	154.22	1.83
Services	276.77	230.85	103.35	103.16	246.12	3.82
Aggregate	140.27	115.19	105.31	100.27	121.64	0.82
	(1)	(2)	(3)	(4)	(5)	(6)

* Difficulties in the theoretical definition of government output and thereby in its measurement led us to omit it from the subsequent analysis. The small size and heterogeneity of the other goods industry led to the same decision for it. These accounted for 5.8 per cent of base year (1949) GDP.

NOTES: (2) is (1) adjusted for hours; (5) is product of (2), (3), and (4); (6) is derived from (5).

SOURCES: (1) DBS, *Employment and Payrolls* (annual), *Canada Year Book*. (2) *idem, Man-Hours and Hourly Earnings*, annual, *Canadian Statistical Review*, Dept. of Labour, *Wages and Hours of Labour in Canada*. For several industries, no direct data on hours were available. Using Hood and Scott, *Output, Labour and Capital*, as a guide, we made the following estimates: Agriculture, Transportation, etc. and Electric Power assume same rate of decline as in Manufacturing, Finance, etc., same rate of decline as in Construction, Trade, mean of hours decline in Services and in Manufacturing. (3) Same as for (4) except for 1931 when no data were available. Thus we extrapolated 1941 backwards to 1937. (4) Census Volumes: 1931, VII, 670; 1941, VII, 516; 1951, IV, Table 19, Estimates for 1937 and 1961, by interpolation and extrapolation.

TABLE B-19

TEST FOR REVISED RESIDUAL CONTRIBUTION
TEN SECTORS, CANADA, 1937-61

Industry	Growth of output			Growth of inputs			Residual contrib.
	Rate	Share	Contribution	Rate	Share	Contribution	
	%	%		%	%		
Agriculture	1.18	11.37	0.134	−0.42	24.94	−0.104	0.238
Forestry	1.75	2.81	0.049	0.24	3.48	0.009	0.040
Mining	5.44	3.44	0.187	3.26	2.55	0.083	0.104
Manufacturing	5.22	29.02	1.514	2.57	23.36	0.600	0.914
Construction	5.68	6.77	0.384	3.56	5.00	0.178	0.206
Electric power	8.36	1.75	0.146	5.05	1.71	0.086	0.060
Trade	4.72	15.45	0.729	3.31	12.34	0.408	0.321
Finance	4.54	9.69	0.440	3.58	4.28	0.154	0.286
Transportation	5.31	8.88	0.471	1.99	7.30	0.145	0.326
Service	3.85	10.83	0.417	3.79	15.03	0.567	−0.152
	(1)	(2)	(3)	(4)	(5)	(6)	(7)

SOURCES: (1), Table 14. (2), Table B-14, (2). (3), (1) times (2); (4), Table B-17, (5) and (7). (5), Table B-17, (6). (6), (4) times (5); (7), (3) minus (6).

TABLE B-20

TEST FOR REVISED RESIDUAL CONTRIBUTION
SEVEN SECTORS, CANADA, 1937-61
(percentages)

Industry *	Labour	Man-hours	Education	Age-sex	Adjusted	Growth rate
						%
Agriculture	51.61	44.05	102.37	104.65	47.62	−1.77
Forestry	76.00	70.38	102.54	98.34	70.97	−1.07
Mining	132.84	109.09	104.52	99.05	112.94	0.51
Manufacturing	193.02	164.63	102.73	100.89	170.94	2.25
Construction	232.70	220.60	103.05	95.77	217.71	3.30
Electric power	278.89	238.03	104.40	96.68	240.24	3.72
Trade	231.60	195.35	104.50	98.91	201.93	2.97
Finance	249.01	230.41	107.96	94.82	235.87	3.64
Transportation	180.39	153.73	103.64	96.80	154.22	1.83
Services	276.77	230.85	103.35	103.16	246.12	3.82
Aggregate	140.27	115.19	105.31	100.27	121.64	0.82
	(1)	(2)	(3)	(4)	(5)	(6)

SOURCES: (1), Table 14. (2), Table B-14; (3), (1) times (2); (4), Table B-17; (5), Table B-17; (6), (4) times (5); (7), (3) minus (6).

APPENDIX C

CONTRIBUTION OF INTER-INDUSTRY SHIFTS, UNITED STATES, 1929-57

There are two basic series on output by industry for the United States between 1929 and 1957. One is Kendrick's which uses prices of 1929.[1] However, his data go to 1957 in three sectors only: agriculture, mining, and manufacturing. A more complete series, covering all sectors for the required period, is that of US Department of Commerce which uses 1954 prices.[2] We present these two sets of data transformed into growth rates in Table C-1.

TABLE C-1
GROWTH RATES OF OUTPUT, US, 1929-57
(percentages)

Industry	Average annual rates of growth	
	Kendrick	Commerce
Agriculture	(net) 0.94	0.97
Mining	1.51	1.57
Manufacturing	3.54	3.47
Construction	—	2.44
Trade	—	2.68
Transportation	—	3.34
Communic'n and Public Util.	—	5.75
Services	—	2.39
Government Enterprises	—	4.12
	(1)	(2)

NOTE: (—) indicates series not available up to 1957.
SOURCES: (1) Kendrick, *Productivity Trends in the United States*, 364, Table B-I, C-II, 398, D-I, 464; (2), see Appendix C, n. 2.

We have decided to use Kendrick's series for the first three sectors in order to keep as much of our analysis in 1929 prices as is possible, especially since most of our capital estimates are so priced. For transportation, communications, and public utilities, it is necessary to use the Dept. of Commerce estimates. The fact that the two series are so similar for the first three industries suggests that no significant bias will result from this. It is necessary to combine the separate series for transportation and for communications and public utilities because of the non-separable capital stock data. The combined sector shows an average annual rate of growth of 4.14 per cent, which is obtained by taking the value of output in 1929 in each, estimating the 1957 output in constant dollars in each using their respective growth rates, totalling the 1929 and the 1957 values in the two sectors, and deriving the rate of growth implicit in these totals.

The basis of the labour input series are Kendrick's man-hour data.[3] The structure of the labour force in terms of age and sex by industry is determined from the following publications: for 1950, the 1950 Census of Population, *Bulletin* P-CI, Table 132, p. 286; for 1930, Social Science Research Council, Committee on Social Security, *Labor Supply in the United States*, by W. S. Woytinsky, 1936, 4, Table IV A. The weighting scheme for standardizing labour input for differences in age and sex is obtained from the 1940 Census of Population publication *Labor Force Sample Statistics: Wage or Salary Income in 1939* (March 1940), 99, Table 6.

To adjust for the changing education achievements of the labour force, we used Professor Houthakker's weights.[4] As the primary data on the structure of the labour force in terms of amount of education received are not given on an industrial basis but only on an occupational one for the censuses prior to 1950, it was necessary to revise the latter classification scheme to approximate an industrial distribution.[5]

We assumed that the growth rate for these two components of quality over the period observed holds for the entire span 1929-57. The effect of these adjustments on the labour input series can be seen in Tables C-2 and C-3.

TABLE C-2

LABOUR INPUT ADJUSTED FOR CHANGES IN QUALITY, US
(millons of man-hours)

Industry	Raw			Adjusted		
	1929	1948	1957	1929	1948	1957
Agriculture	25,474	18,828	12,445	25,474	22,354	16,042
Mining	2,313	2,056	1,672	2,313	2,169	1,809
Manufacturing	24,290	32,278	34,438	24,290	32,403	35,604
Construction	5,304	6,890	8,575	5,304	7,174	9,100
Trade	23,555	27,334	30,106	23.555	27,593	30,507
T. C. and P. Ut.	10,466	10,194	9,586	10,466	10,393	9,863
Services *	21,971	20,515	24,298	21,971	24,987	32,353

* Includes Finance, Insurance, and Real Estate. Excludes Government and Government Enterprises.

TABLE C-3

INDEXES OF QUALITY CHANGE, US
(1929 = 100)

Industry	Age-sex changes		Increased education	
	1948	1957	1948	1957
Agriculture	113.59	120.77	104.52	106.74
Mining	103.50	105.20	101.91	102.83
Manufacturing	103.22	104.88	102.56	103.80
Construction	99.99	99.99	104.13	106.14
Trade	97.12	95.72	103.94	105.86
T. C. and P. Ut.	101.62	102.40	100.33	100.48
Services	106.88	110.31	113.62	120.71

There is no single source of capital stock data by industry for the United States covering the period 1929-57. However, there are independent estimates for the different sectors, from which we have obtained our series.

For agriculture, we have Kendrick's estimates of the value in 1929 prices, of the stock of structures and machinery and equipment for 1929 and 1953.[6] The Dept. of Commerce has also estimated these two components for 1929, 1953, and 1957, in 1954 prices.[7] The Kendrick estimates indicate an over-all increase of 45.6 per cent between 1929 and 1953, while the Commerce series increases by 42.9 per cent over the same period. The latter increases by a further 5.0 per cent between 1953 and 1957. The similarity of these results for the earlier period, and the brevity of the later period have led us to project the Kendrick figure as of 1953 up to 1957 by the increase in the Commerce series.

The Kendrick estimates for manufacturing increase by 53.7 per cent between 1929 and 1953, and the Commerce data show a similar increase of 51.1 per cent.[8] We therefore have projected the Kendrick figure for 1953 by the increase of 16.9 per cent in the Commerce series for 1953-7 to obtain a 1957 stock estimate.

Capital stock in mining decreased by 10.5 per cent from 1929 to 1953 according to Kendrick's estimates for structures and machinery and equipment.[9] To project his 1953 net stock estimate to 1957, it was necessary to calculate net investment in mining for 1954 through 1957. Taking the gross investment figures in current dollars in this sector for this period[10] we deflate them by the implicit deflator for aggregate investment.[11] Setting 1929 equal to 100 in this series allows us to arithmetically convert the gross investment in 1954 prices into 1929 prices. These gross investment figures are put onto a net basis by weighting them by the mean of the 1954 and 1955 ratios of net capital formation to gross capital formation in the aggregate economy.[12] Adding these net investment data in 1929 prices to the net stock existing at the end of 1953, also in prices of 1929, gives us a net stock figure for 1957.

A similar procedure is followed for the fourth sector, transportation, communication, and public utilities. We use Goldsmith's[13] updating of Ulmer's estimates[14] to obtain the increase in capital between 1929 and 1956. Net investment for 1957 in 1929 prices is calculated in the same way as was done in the case of mining, thereby enabling us to estimate the stock in 1957.

For the remaining sectors, no direct estimates of their respective stocks and their growth are available. However, since these industries together comprise the remainder of the private domestic economy, we can estimate the capital stock in an indirect fashion, by removing from the total private stock the amount of capital contained in the preceding four sectors.

TABLE C-4

CAPITAL STOCK BY INDUSTRY, US, 1929, 1948, AND 1957
(in billions of 1929 dollars)

Industry	1929	1948	1957
Agriculture	17.5	21.1	26.8
Mining	7.6	6.7	7.3
Manufacturing	23.3	28.1	41.9
T. C. and Pub. Ut.	43.9	45.3	63.4
Total, 4 sectors	92.3	101.2	139.4
Total private stock *	257.8	271.8	446.3
Residual stock	165.5	170.6	306.9

* Kendrick, *Productivity Trends in the United States*, 323, Table A-XVI, structures, machinery, and equipment.

Table C-4 gives the estimates of capital stock by sector for the US economy.
For estimating inter-industry shifts, we require the income per standardized
man-hour of labour input in some base year. We have chosen 1948 as that year,
because of the availability of input data by which the income estimates must be
divided. The factor coefficients are also estimated from the distribution of income in 1948, because of the high level of economic activity prevailing then.
The Tables C-5 to C-8 prepare the data for the measures of inter-industry effects.

TABLE C-5

NATIONAL INCOME BY INDUSTRY, US, 1948

(in 1929 prices)

Industry	National income 1929 millions of dollars	Output in 1948 (1929 = 100)	National income 1948 millions of dollars
Agriculture	8,083	119.2	9,635
Mining	2,048	133.3	2,730
Manufacturing	21,888	184.2	40,318
Construction	3,808	132.3	5,038
Trade	13,358	167.3	22,348
Transportation	6,636	211.8	21,201
Communications and public utilities	2,864	249.5	30,401
Services	23,031	132.0	
	(1)	(2)	(3)

SOURCES: (1), Dept. of Commerce, *Income and Output*, 130, Table I-10; (2), Kendrick,
Productivity Trends in the United States, 302-3, Table A-IV; (3), (1) times (2).

TABLE C-6

INCOME PER UNIT OF LABOUR AND CAPITAL, US, 1948

Industry	Labour share	Labour income	Capital income	Average income	
				Labour *	Capital †
	%	mill. $	mill. $	$	%
Agriculture	85.4	8,229	1,406	0.368	0.067
Mining	71.2	1,945	785	0.897	0.117
Manufacturing	72.7	29,311	11,007	0.905	0.392
Construction	93.1	4,689	349	0.654	‡
Trade	82.0	18,332	4,016	0.664	‡
Transportation, communications, and public utilities	79.2	16,791	4,410	1.616	0.097
Services	75.0	22,795	7,606	0.912	‡
	(1)	(2)	(3)	(4)	(5)

* Dollars per standardized man-hour.
† Dollars per dollar of capital.
‡ Single estimates for these industries are not available. The rate of return to them as an
aggregate is 7.02 per cent for capital, and for their labour, taken together, the compensation
per standard man-hour is $0.767.
SOURCES: (1), Dept. of Commerce, *Income and Output*, 200, Table VI-1, 203, Table VI-5,
and 210, Table VI-12, all for 1948; (2), (1) times Table C-5 (3); (3), Table C-5, (3) minus (2),
C-6; (4), (2) plus Table C-2 (5); (5), (3) plus Table C-4 (2).

TABLE C-7
Factor Inputs in Labour Equivalents, US, 1929-57

| Industry | Weights for capital | Factor inputs in millions of standard man-hours | | | |
| | | Capital | | Total factors | |
		1929	1957	1929	1957
Agriculture	0.181	3,167	4,850	28,641	20,892
Mining	0.131	993	954	3,306	2,763
Manufacturing	0.433	10,089	18,144	34,379	53,748
Transportation, communications, and public utilities	0.060	2,645	3,802	13,111	13,683
Others	0.092	15,143	28,081	65,973	100,041
	(1)	(2)	(3)	(4)	(5)

SOURCES: (1), Table C-6 (5) plus (4); (2), (1) times Table C-4 (1); (3), (1) times Table C-4 (3); (4), (2) plus Table C-2 (4); (5), (3) plus Table C-2 (6).

TABLE C-8
Test for Revised Residual Contribution
Five Sectors, US, 1929-57
(percentages)

| Industry | Growth of output | | | Growth of input | | | Residual contribution |
	Rate	Share	Contribution	Rate	Share	Contribution	
Agriculture	0.94	7.32	0.069	−0.86	16.12	−0.138	0.207
Mining	1.51	2.07	0.031	−0.54	1.88	−0.010	0.041
Manufacturing	3.34	30.62	1.084	1.61	27.45	0.442	0.642
Transportation, communications, and public utilities	4.14	16.10	0.667	0.15	8.08	0.012	0.655
Others	2.63	43.89	1.154	1.51	46.67	0.702	0.452
	(1)	(2)	(3)	(4)	(5)	(6)	(7)

SOURCES: (1), Table C-1; (2), Table C-5; (3), (1) times (2); (4), Table C-7; (5), Tables C-2, C-4, and C-6 for conversion to labour equivalents; (6), (4) times (5); (7), (3) minus (6).

APPENDIX D

DIS-AGGREGATION OF THE MANUFACTURING SECTOR, UNITED STATES, 1929-57

THE OUTPUT DATA for these sectors are obtained directly from Kendrick's Table D-IV, and are consequently not reproduced here.

The labour input series commences with Kendrick's man-hour figures for 1948.[1] These are projected to 1929 and 1957 on the basis of his indexes given in Table D-IV.[2] The adjustments for age and sex, and for education exactly parallel those described in Appendix C for the broader industrial groupings. Tables D-1 and D-2 present the basic labour series.

TABLE D-1

LABOUR INPUT IN MANUFACTURING, ADJUSTED FOR QUALITY,
US, 1929, 1948, AND 1957

Subsector	Raw man-hours	(millions)		Adjusted man-hours	(millions)	
	1929	1948	1957	1929	1948	1957
Food	2,590	3,243	3,006	2,590	3,409	3,235
Textiles	4,613	4,850	4,017	4,613	5,130	4,363
Leather	856	764	693	856	782	718
Rubber	420	507	560	420	547	626
Forest products	2,384	2,131	1,802	2,384	2,223	1,918
Paper	773	1,006	1,158	773	1,070	1,268
Printing	1,453	1,627	1,855	1,453	1,613	1,830
Chemicals	864	1,382	1,643	864	1,549	1,944
Petroleum	346	440	418	346	480	475
Stone, clay	922	1,238	1,277	922	1,267	1,321
Primary metals	1,743	2,297	2,343	1,743	2,393	2,489
Fabricated metals	1,589	2,339	2,766	1,589	2,532	3,109
Non-electric machinery	2,487	4,041	4,447	2,487	4,131	4,594
Electric machinery	1,089	1,706	2,382	1,089	1,739	2,450
Transportation equipment	1,523	2,379	3,784	1,523	2,491	4,049
Miscellaneous and instruments	638	968	1,082	638	1,047	1,215
	(1)	(2)	(3)	(4)	(5)	(6)

Kendrick does not present sufficiently refined capital stock data for our purposes. Such data are provided by Goldsmith for 1929, 1948, and 1956.[3] With no estimates for 1957 available at the required level of detail, we projected the 1929-56 growth rate for one year. The estimates for 1929, 1948, and 1957 are given in Table D-3. It should be noted that the last six items have been derived from the total, "metal and its products", given by Goldsmith and distributed by the shares of these items in this category as estimated by Kendrick[4] (Tables D-4 to D-6).

TABLE D-2

INDEXES OF QUALITY CHANGE, MANUFACTURING, US

(1929 = 100)

Subsector	Age-sex changes		Increased education	
	1948	1957	1948	1957
Food	103.38	105.02	101.68	102.48
Textiles	104.71	107.02	101.01	101.49
Leather	100.43	100.64	101.97	102.92
Rubber	106.15	109.19	101.59	102.35
Forest products	102.40	103.55	101.90	102.80
Paper	104.62	106.88	101.66	102.46
Printing	96.98	95.52	102.20	103.26
Chemicals	108.21	112.33	103.60	105.35
Petroleum	104.89	107.30	104.02	105.98
Stone, clay	100.08	100.11	102.26	103.34
Primary metals	103.36	104.99	100.79	101.17
Fabricated metals	103.36	104.99	104.75	107.07
Non-electric machinery	99.94	99.91	102.30	103.40
Electric machinery	99.94	99.91	101.98	102.93
Transportation equipment	100.83	101.23	103.83	105.71
Miscellaneous and instruments	104.31	106.41	103.71	105.51

TABLE D-3

NET CAPITAL IN THE SUBSECTORS OF MANUFACTURING, US,

1929, 1948, AND 1957

Subsector	Stock (millions of 1929 dollars)		
	1929	1948	1957
Food, beverages, and tobacco	4.54	4.38	5.22
Textiles and apparel	3.34	2.37	2.39
Leather and products	0.31	0.18	0.15
Rubber products	0.49	0.47	0.60
Forest products incl. lumber, and furniture	2.26	1.64	1.66
Paper and allied products	1.36	1.53	2.48
Printing and publishing	1.05	1.13	1.43
Chemicals and allied products	1.73	3.32	7.89
Petroleum and coal products	4.02	7.23	9.31
Stone, clay, and glas products	1.70	1.17	1.73
Primary metal industries	2.70	3.90	6.60
Fabricated metal products	1.10	1.80	3.10
Non-electrical machinery	2.40	2.30	4.00
Electrical machinery	1.20	1.50	2.50
Transportation equipment	2.00	2.80	4.90
Miscellaneous and instruments	0.70	0.80	1.30
	(1)	(2)	(3)

TABLE D-4

NATIONAL INCOME BY SUBSECTOR OF MANUFACTURING, US, 1948

(in 1929 prices)

Subsector	National income 1929 millions of dollars	Output in 1948 (1929 = 100)	National income 1948 millions of dollars
Food	2,135	154.5	3,299
Tobacco	256	185.8	476
Textiles	1,796	161.5	2,900
Apparel	1,262	154.0	1,944
Leather	602	119.5	719
Rubber	355	170.2	604
Lumber	852	103.2	877
Furniture	676	158.4	1,077
Paper	562	198.2	1,114
Printing	1,589	146.2	2,323
Chemicals	1,129	309.8	3,498
Petroleum	917	201.2	1,845
Stone, clay	799	177.6	1,419
Primary metals	2,174 °	161.3	3,507
Fabricated metals	1,440 °	181.4	2,612
Non-electric machinery	1,890	218.9	4,137
Electric machinery	1,045	251.9	2,634
Transportation equipment	1,700	163.7	2,783
Miscellaneous and instruments	709 °	226.4	1,605
	(1)	(2)	(3)

° These three subsectors do not exist in the 1929 classification scheme. We took the 1948 proportions, projected these back to 1929 along their respective output indexes, and thereby obtained the 1929 proportions within the metal and metal products total for that year.

SOURCES: As for Table C-5, except (2) which is from Kendrick, *Productivity Trends in the United States*, 468-75, Table D-IV.

TABLE D-5

INCOME PER UNIT OF LABOUR AND CAPITAL:

SUBSECTORS OF MANUFACTURING, US, 1948

Subsector	Labour share	Labour income	Capital income	Income per unit Labour	Capital
	%	mill. $	mill. $	$	$
Food	73.0	2,755	1,019	0.808	0.233
Textiles	78.7	3,812	1,032	0.743	0.435
Leather	88.3	635	84	0.812	0.468
Rubber	79.8	482	122	0.881	0.260
Forest	80.4	1,571	383	0.707	0.234
Paper	66.8	744	370	0.695	0.242
Printing	82.3	1,912	411	1.185	0.364
Chemicals	61.7	2,158	1,340	1.393	0.403
Petroleum	32.2	594	1,251	1.238	0.173
Stone, clay	75.0	1,064	355	0.840	0.303
Primary metals	71.5	2,507	999	1.048	0.256
Fabricated metals	76.9	2,009	603	0.793	0.335
Non-electric machinery	76.2	3,153	985	0.763	0.428
Electric machinery	77.5	2,040	592	1.173	0.395
Transportation equipment	70.7	1,968	815	0.790	0.291
Miscellaneous and instruments	80.5	1,292	313	1.234	0.391
	(1)	(2)	(3)	(4)	(5)

SOURCES: (1), See Table C-6 (1); (2), (1) times Table D-4 (3); (3), Table D-4 (3) minus Table D-5 (2); (4), (2) + Table D-1 (5); (5), (3) + Table D-3 (2).

TABLE D-6
Factor Inputs in Labour Equivalents:
Subsectors of Manufacturing, US, 1929 and 1957

| Subsector | Weights for capital | Factor inputs in millions of standard man-hours | | | |
| | | Capital | | Total factors | |
		1929	1957	1929	1957
Food	0.288	1,307	1,503	3,897	4,738
Textiles	0.586	1,957	1,400	6,570	5,763
Leather	0.576	178	86	1,034	804
Rubber	0.295	144	177	564	803
Forest	0.330	747	549	3,131	2,467
Paper	0.348	473	862	1,246	2,130
Printing	0.307	322	439	1,775	2,269
Chemicals	0.290	501	2,285	1,365	4,229
Petroleum	0.140	562	1,301	908	1,776
Stone, clay	0.361	614	624	1,536	1,945
Primary metals	0.245	660	1,614	2.403	4,103
Fabricated metals	0.423	465	1,310	2,054	4,419
Non-electric machinery	0.561	1,346	2,244	3,833	6,838
Electric machinery	0.337	404	841	1,493	3,291
Transportation equipment	0.369	737	1,807	2,260	5,856
Miscellaneous and instruments	0.317	222	412	860	1,627
	(1)	(2)	(3)	(4)	(5)

Sources: (1), Table D-5 (5) plus (4); (2), (1) times Table D-3 (1); (3), (1) times Table D-3 (3); (4), (2) plus Table D-1 (4); (5), (3) plus Table D-1 (6).

APPENDIX E

ECONOMIC GROWTH SINCE 1890, UNITED STATES AND CANADA

I. UNITED STATES

THE LABOUR INPUT is based on Kendrick's man-hour estimates to which we have already referred.[1] The quality adjustments involve some simple estimation techniques, because of the lack of comprehensive data for the earlier years. The age-sex distribution for 1909 was calculated from the 1940 Census of Population document, *Comparative Occupation Statistics for the United States, 1870-1940* (159, Tables 14 and 15). As the industrial groupings were slightly different from our previous 1930 estimates, we recalculated the latter to make it strictly comparable with the 1910 distribution, the data for this being given in the same document. As for education, there is no industrial data available prior to 1940. We calculated the relative increase between 1910 and 1930 as compared to that of 1929-57 for the total economy, as given by Denison,[2] and, assuming that the rate of increase within each sector from the early period to the later matched that of the total economy, applied the latters's rate of increase to the industrial data of Table C-3, column four. This ratio was 46.04 per cent of the later periods increase.[3]

For 1889, we also lack industrial data on age-sex composition by industry. Denison does have an estimate of the increase in output occasioned by the changes in these variables for the total economy between 1890 and 1910. Taking the ratio of this increase to that of 1910-30, we apply it to the 1910-30 increase within each industry.[4] The education item was calculated as above, using the estimated increase for 1910 through 1920 as representative of each of the two preceding decades, and dividing this by the 1940-50 increase to obtain a ratio by which we can weight the industrial increases due to education between 1940 and 1950.[5]

While these estimates are far from satisfactory, the fact that both the elements

TABLE E-1

INDEXES OF QUALITY CHANGE, LONG RUN, US
(1929 = 100)

Industry	Age-sex changes		Increased education	
	1889	1909	1889	1909
Agriculture	82.86	89.91	94.23	96.99
Mining	88.39	92.65	97.50	98.72
Manufacturing	89.85	93.57	96.67	98.28
Construction	89.28	93.21	94.72	97.25
Trade	100.83	100.53	94.95	97.37
Transportation, communications, and public utilities	96.07	97.51	99.57	99.78
Services	107.62	104.83	84.03	91.30
	(1)	(2)	(3)	(4)

—age-sex composition and education—were much less significant as contributors to the growth rate in the early period means that our figures will not be seriously biased. The levels of the two indexes for each of these years are given in Table E-1.

The labour input series in standardized man-hours can now be calculated and this is done in Table E-2.

TABLE E-2

LABOUR INPUT ADJUSTED FOR CHANGES IN QUALITY, LONG RUN, US

Industry	Millions of raw man-hours		Millions of std. man-hours	
	1889	1909	1889	1909
Agriculture	21,045	24,656	16,431	21,502
Mining	1,198	2,342	1,032	2,142
Manufacturing	11,264	20,365	9,783	18,727
Construction	2,596	4,001	2,195	3,627
Trade	7,677	13,310	7,350	13,028
Transportation, communications, and public utilities	5,123	9,737	4,901	9,474
Services	9,333	15,710	8,440	15,036
	(1)	(2)	(3)	(4)

The capital stock estimates are derived by projecting our 1929 figures by means of Kendrick's indexes for the various industries. Estimates for construction, trade, and services are derived as a residual, following the procedure of Table C-4. The same conversion factor for expressing capital input in terms of labour equivalents is used. Tables E-3 to E-5 give the required information.

TABLE E-3

CAPITAL INPUT OVER LONG RUN, US
(in millions of 1929 dollars)

Industry	Net stock	
	1889	1909
Agriculture	8,233	14,267
Mining	904	3,248
Manufacturing	4,101	12,675
Transportation	13,568	20,538
Communications and public utilities	1,792	7,447
Total, four sectors	28,588	58,175
Total private stock	62,378	155,392
Residual stock	33,790	97,217
	(1)	(2)

SOURCES: Kendrick, *Productivity Trends in the United States*, Agric., 367. Table B-3; Mining, 394, Table C-21; Mfg., 464, Table D-1; Transport, 540, Table G-1; Comm. and P. Ut., 580, Table H-1; Total Private, 323, Table A-XVI. See Goldsmith, *The National Wealth of the United States in the Postwar Period*, 77. Table 17, for separation of transport from comm. and p. ut.

TABLE E-4

FACTOR INPUTS IN LABOUR EQUIVALENTS, LONG RUN, US

Industry	Weights for capital	Factor inputs in millions of standard man-hours			
		Capital		Total factors	
		1889	1909	1889	1909
Agriculture	0.181	1,488	2,582	17,919	24,084
Mining	0.131	118	425	1,150	2,567
Manufacturing	0.433	1,776	5,488	11,559	24,215
Transportation, communications, and public utilities	0.060	922	1,679	5,823	11,153
Others	0.092	3,109	8,944	21,094	40,635
	(1)	(2)	(3)	(4)	(5)

NOTE: For method, see Table C-7.

TABLE E-5

DISTRIBUTION OF INPUTS TO DERIVE INTER-INDUSTRY SHIFTS, OVER THE LONG RUN, US

Industrie	Weights	Share in standardized labour			
		1889	1909	1929	1957
		%	%	%	%
(a)					
Agriculture	0.368	32.78	25.74	22.28	11.86
Mining	0.897	2.06	2.56	2.02	1.34
Manufacturing	0.905	19.51	22.42	21.26	26.32
Construction	0.654	4.38	4.34	4.64	6.73
Trade	0.664	14.66	15.60	20.60	22.55
Transportation, communications, and public utilities	1.616	19.78	11.34	9.15	7.29
Services	0.912	16.84	18.00	20.05	23.92
	(1)	(2)	(3)	(4)	(5)

		Share in total input			
		%	%	%	%
(b)					
Agriculture		31.14	23.46	19.70	10.93
Mining		2.00	2.50	2.27	1.45
Manufacturing		20.09	23.59	23.64	28.12
Construction		○	○	○	○
Trade		○	○	○	○
Transportation, communications, and public utilities		10.12	10.86	9.02	7.16
Services		○	○	○	○
		(1)	(2)	(3)	(4)

NOTE: The combined share of these three industries in total input was: 1889, 36.66 per cent; 1909, 39.58 per cent; 1929, 45.37 per cent; 1957, 52.34 per cent.

SOURCES: (a) (1), Table C-6 (4); (2), Table E-2 (3); (3), Table E-2 (4); (4) Table 35 (2); (5), Table 35 (3).

(b) (1), Table E-4 (4); (2), Table E-4 (5); (3), Table 35 (5).

Derivation of Long-Run Factor Coefficients, US

For the five sector grouping, we used Kendrick's weights for the total private domestic economy.[6] His 1899-1909 weights were used for our early period, and are 65 for labour and 35 for capital. His 1909-19 and 1919-29 weights were averaged to give a labour coefficient of 69.5 and a capital coefficient of 30.5 in the middle period. For the final one, we used the coefficients implicit in Table C-6.

The weights for the four sector grouping were derived from the relevant industry weights given by Kendrick.[7] These weights are 70.9 and 29.1 for 1889-1909 and 72.9 and 27.1 for 1909-29.

For the individual industries in the early periods, the labour coefficients are as follows:

	1889-1909	1909-29
Agriculture	0.631	0.565
Mining	0.700	0.700
Manufacturing	0.768	0.768
Transportation, communications, and public utilities	0.743	0.756
Other	0.650	0.695

II. CANADA
TABLE E-6
Long-Run Labour Input in Canada

	1890	1910	1926
Labour force (thousands)	1675	2801	3671
Annual hours	2960	2795	2600
Man-hours (millions)	4958	7829	9545

Source: Colin Clark, *Conditions of Economic Progress*, 108-9, Table XIV. As no data were available for 1891, we had to use the 1890 figures to estimate the growth of labour input over a twenty-year period.

TABLE E-7
Long-Run Capital Input in Canada
(millions 1949 dollars)

	1891	1910	1926
Residential construction	2,054	4,158	6,486
Business capital	5,296	11,406	14,303
Total stock	7,350	15,564	20,789

Sources: For residential construction a rough estimate of the 1867 stock was made by applying the value per dwelling in 1921 to the number of dwellings in 1867, as given in Firestone, *Canada's Economic Development*, 85, Table 19. This enabled an estimate of annual retirements in subsequent years; and by decumulating from our 1926 stock estimate using our investment data, we were able to calculate these estimates. For business capital our industrial stock data enabled us to estimate the capital-labour ratio in the various components of the business sector. Using Firestone's distribution of labour by industry (184, Table 65), and weighting these by the capital-labour ratio gave us a rough estimate of capital in the business sector.

APPENDIX F

GEOMETRIC AND ARITHMETIC INDEXES

OUR COBB-DOUGLAS FUNCTION expressed in terms of growth rates is based on a geometric combination of inputs. To retain consistency, outputs should also be combined geometrically. Since most data are not presented in this way by the various statistical agencies, it is important to see the bias that results from the pure arithmetic approach. We cannot compare the latter to a pure geometric combination since the primary data available—those at the industry level—are based on arithmetic combinations of more detailed data. We can present a mixed index, which is geometrically combined at the industry level only. These have been derived as a by-product of our study of inter-industry shifts, and are compared to the pure arithmetic series which we have used in the study (Table F-1).

TABLE F-1

GROWTH RATES OF OUTPUT USING DIFFERENT INDEXES

(percentages)

Type of aggregate	Arithmetic	Geometric
Ten sector, Canada	4.54	4.47
Seven sector, Canada	4.49	4.52

SOURCE: Tables 26, 27, 31, and 32

In both cases, the bias is very slight. The only effect is to lower the residual from 2.41 to 2.34 percentage points in the ten sector case, thereby approximating the test residual of 2.34 percentage points very closely, and to raise that of the seven sector case to 2.94 percentage points, once more approximating the test residual of 3.06 somewhat closer than the residual based on the arithmetic combination which was 2.91.

None of our conclusions are seriously affected by this change, and it remains for the reader to choose either the pure arithmetic or the mixed index as being most meaningful in the absence of a pure geometric index. Our choice of the former was based on a desire to retain concepts that are generally understood and widely used.[1]

APPENDIX G

FOREIGN INFLUENCE ON CANADIAN ECONOMIC GROWTH

EXCEPT FOR THE SECOND CHAPTER, where we evaluated the net effect of international trade by considering international capital flows, no attempt has been made to estimate the importance of the foreign sector in Canadian economic growth. This stems from the nature of our model, which does not permit explicit inclusion of the two components of trade—exports and imports.[1] In our treatment of industrial growth, we have used the domestic rather than the national framework, and have been compelled, as a result, to omit the effect of foreign capital as well as the role of trade itself.

These omissions are unfortunate, insofar as the Canadian economy is greatly oriented towards foreign trade and foreign capital inflows. The former has accounted for between 20 and 25 per cent of national product for many years, and the latter has been responsible for a large and increasing share of net capital formation, particularly in the post-war years. As a result, we intend to supplement our preceding analysis with a brief survey of these very important factors.

There have been few studies considering the contribution of exports and imports to economic growth in quantitative terms. Most of the discussion has been impressionistic, leaving the evaluation of these contributions in a nebulous state. While not being able to remedy this neglect, we do feel that an impression of the orders of magnitude can be obtained. From the inter-industry table for 1949 it is possible to derive the proportion of final output by industry that is exported, and the importance of imports relative to total input in the various industries in 1949 (Table G-1).

TABLE G-1

INDUSTRIAL DISTRIBUTION OF IMPORTS AND EXPORTS, CANADA, 1949

Industry	Exports as % of final demand	Imports as % of total inputs
Agriculture	46.2	1.1
Forestry, etc.	117.1 *	0.4
Mining	90.9	5.0
Manufacturing	26.0	13.2
Construction	‡	3.8
Electric power and gas	3.2	0.8
Finance, etc.	‡	‡
Transport, etc. and trade	17.6	2.3
Services †	0.1	1.9

* Large percentage is due to inventory disinvestment.
† Includes public administration and defence.
‡ Negligible.
SOURCE: DBS, *Supplement to the Inter-Industry Flow of Goods and Services, Canada, 1949*, Table 1.

The great concentration of exports in the primary industries is a well-known aspect of Canadian trade, particularly as expounded in the staple theory. The high proportions in manufacturing and transportation reflect a transient situation in which Canada was aiding in the reconstruction of Europe, and filling the void in world trade created by the ravages of the war. The most serious problem with such a table is that it is static. Nevertheless, the same general impression as to the industrial distribution of exports is conveyed when other years are examined. For instance, in 1961, the distribution of exports among the main exporting sectors was as follows (Table G-2).

TABLE G-2

INDUSTRIAL DISTRIBUTION OF EXPORTS, CANADA, 1961
(millions of current dollars)

Sector	Value of exports
Farm and fish products	1,301
Forest products	1,623
Other manufactures	719
Metals and minerals	1,863
Total exports	5,896

SOURCE: Bank of Canada, *Statistical Summary, Supplement*, 1961, 152-3.

Again we see the focus of export demand is on primary products. What is significant is the large proportion that is concentrated on the slow growing farm, fishing, and forestry industries. Foreign demand has not been able to make these sectors major contributors to the high growth rate of aggregate output. Indirect or linkage effects have no doubt entered to stimulate both processing and supply industries in the manufacturing sector, and a dynamic inter-industry model would be of great use in seeing how extensive these have been. Also, the much more complicated process of providing foreign exchange for the acquisition of materials and capital in the rapidly growing sectors should be considered. Nevertheless, the existence of foreign demand may have had a negative effect on the growth rate by reducing the mobility of factors of production out of the slow growing industries and into the more rapidly growing, higher productivity industries.

Mining is the one exception to the concentration of foreign demand on slowly growing primary industries. The high growth rate has been coupled with a very large export share in output. Together with the great influx of foreign capital into this sector, these elements reinforce our thesis that mining is best considered as an extension of the United States economy. To keep the impact of foreigners on the over-all growth rate, as transmitted through mining, in perspective, however, we must recall the small weight mining has in the total structure of production. To treat mining as a leading sector in Canadian economic growth, as exponents of the staple theory tend to do for the post-war years, is to neglect the relative size of that industry.

Turning to imports, we find that they have been rather minor as a portion of total inputs when materials alone are considered, with the exception of manufacturing. The bulk of imports are channelled to consumption and investment. In 1949,

6.2 per cent of consumption by Canadians consisted of foreign goods and services, and this element has remained important to the present. While it may be argued that this importation has substituted for domestic production, which otherwise might have served to augment the growth rate, the whole concept of the gains from trade is ignored. In fact, it may be argued that foreign goods have created markets into which Canadian producers have subsequently entered and benefited thereby. Suffice it to say that no simple summary of the importance of imports by Canadian consumers for the growth rate is possible. It is hoped that foreign trade analysts will devote more effort to investigating the impact of these imports on the growth rate.

The one type of import that has been dealt with at great length in the literature, and which has been studied in detail by government agencies, is capital. This has entered at an ever-increasing rate, as can be expected from the much more rapid growth of imports than of exports. Between 1937 and 1961, imports in constant dollars grew at an annual rate of 4.79 per cent while exports increased much slower at 3.90 per cent.[2] The nature of the data does not permit a measurement of the proportion of capital formation by industry that has been a result of capital inflows, but some data are available on the role of foreign financing of aggregate capital formation (Table G-3).

TABLE G-3

FOREIGN FINANCING OF CANADIAN INVESTMENT, 1946-60

Foreign financing as % of	1946-49	1950-55	1956-60
Gross capital formation	19	25	33
Net capital formation	24	33	45

SOURCE: DBS, *The Canadian Balance of International Payments, 1960, and International Investment Position*, 49, statement 19.

These data indicate just how important foreign capital has been in Canadian economic growth, given the importance of capital in the process. Our findings in the second chapter no doubt understate the role of foreign investment because of the great amount of reinvestment in Canada of earnings of foreign-owned enterprises. Nor could a model such as ours separately account for the flow of technical knowledge that has accompanied foreign capital into Canada, the productivity of which is included in the ever-increasing residual.

TABLE G-4

CAPITAL IN CANADIAN INDUSTRY OWNED BY NON-RESIDENTS

Industry	Percentage of capital owned by non-residents	
	1939	1959
Manufacturing	43	51
Mining and smelting	38	60
Railways	56	27
Other utilities	29	15
Merchandising and construction	10	9

NOTE: Based on current dollar book values of capital.
SOURCE: *Canadian Balance* (1960 ed.), 84, Table XVI; (1958 ed.), 64, Table XVI.

A picture of the industrial distribution of this foreign capital is given in Table G-4.

The importance of foreign capital in manufacturing—the most important sector in the Canadian economy—together with the increasingly dominant role it has played in mining, and in particular the petroleum industry, is clearly evident in this table. On the other hand, the ownership of railways and utilities has been gradually passing into Canadian hands. Nevertheless, as Table G-3 indicated, there is little doubt that since the war, foreign capital has come to play an increasing role in the growth of domestic capital.[3]

One can only conclude, as a result of these findings, that the foreign sector has played its most significant part in the economic growth of Canada by financing the growth in capital. The impact of trade proper remains unknown in quantitative terms, and attempts to estimate it would be a most valuable contribution to our understanding of economic growth.

APPENDIX H

REVISION OF OUTPUT DATA

As was revealed in Chapter III, there has been a substantial upward revision of the Index of Industrial Production (IIP) in 1966. Fortunately, we have been able to incorporate these new data into our study. Nevertheless, it is of interest to consider the magnitude and effects of these revisions.

First, the extent of the change can best be seen in Table II-1.

TABLE H-1
CHANGES IN OUTPUT SERIES BASED ON 1966 REVISION OF IIP, SELECTED YEARS
(Per cent change in level)

Year	Real GDP	IIP	Manufacturing	Mining	Electric power and gas utilities
1956	1.3	3.7	4.2	2.8	−0.2
1961	2.7	7.7	9.1	6.0	−0.4
1965	3.9	10.8	13.3	5.3	—

SOURCE: DBS, *Annual Supplement to the Monthly Index of Industrial Production*, May 1966, 8, Table A.

The effects of these major revisions are clearly significant. One way of evaluating them is to consider the key rates of growth in our study before and after these revisions. These are presented in Table H-2.

TABLE H-2
SELECTED GROWTH RATES COMPARING OLD AND REVISED OUTPUT DATA
CANADA, 1937-61

	Output	Residual
Mining		
Old	5.18	1.92
New	5.44	2.18
Per cent change	5.0	13.5
Manufacturing		
Old	4.84	2.27
New	5.22	2.65
Per cent change	7.9	16.7
GDP (10 Industry Composite)		
Old	4.31	2.84
New	4.54	3.07
Per cent change	5.3	8.1

SOURCE: Tables 19 and 21. For old data, see N. H. Lithwick. "*Economic Growth in Canada, A Quantitative Analysis*," Ph. D. Dissertation, Harvard University, 1963. Table numbers are the same.

This revision, particularly in manufacturing, is on such a major scale that one's view of recent economic growth in Canada must be considerably altered.[1] For example, in its *Second Annual Review* the Economic Council of Canada voiced concern over the slow growth of productivity, defined as output per man, over the period 1960-5. Their concern is largely invalidated by the revision of the output data and by the relatively great inter-industry effect in the period 1950-5, which makes productivity growth in later periods appear to be too low. Table H-3 presents a revision of their estimates with these adjustments taken into account.

TABLE H-3

PRODUCTIVITY GROWTH IN CANADA
BASED ON REVISED DATA, 1950-65

(Average annual percentage change)

	1950-55	1955-60	1960-65
Output per person employed (Economic Council)	3.5	0.9	2.1
Persons employed	1.5	2.1	2.8
Output (Economic Council)	5.0	3.0	4.9
Output (Revised)	5.3	3.8	5.6
Output per person employed (Revised)	3.8	1.7	2.8
Inter-industry shift	0.6	0.1	0.1
Net output per person employed (Revised)	3.2	1.6	2.7

SOURCE: Economic Council of Canada, *Second Annual Review*, Dec. 1965, 15-6, Tables 2.2 and 2.3.

The remaining difference is no doubt due to the very high rate of productivity advance in agriculture in the period 1950-55, which contributes about 0.8 percentage points to total productivity advance in that period as compared to 0.5 percentage points in 1960-5. This reduces the discrepancy in non-agricultural output per man in these two periods to a very minor amount.

These findings reverse the pessimism displayed by the Council both with respect to comparisons with our past performance, and with productivity growth in the US during this same period. In addition, those that have bemoaned our rising unit labour costs as a source of recent inflationary pressures have a much weaker basis for their contention. Rather than rising at an annual rate of 0.4 per cent in manufacturing between 1960-5, they actually have fallen at a rate of 0.7 per cent per year over this period.[2]

What is most disturbing about the revisions, therefore, is not the fact that our recent performance turns out to be quite satisfactory, but that an error of such magnitude could have been made over such a protracted period without being detected. The need for much greater research into the statistical measures of economic performance has never been more dramatically presented. Perhaps the time is ripe for an independent research agency to be established to provide checks on official government data and to undertake the research that the government agencies have been unable to provide.

APPENDIX I

UNITED STATES CAPITAL-STOCK ESTIMATES

For United States capital stock there are two sources of data—J. Kendrick's *Productivity Trends in the United States* and the U.S. Department of Commerce's estimates as published in *The Statistical History of the United States*. Superficially these differ substantially, but when adjusted to the same basis, namely, one that is comparable to the Canadian estimates, they do appear to be very similar.

The Commerce estimates are given for 1956 in 1947–9 dollars.[1] The three major components of their values are:

	(billion dollars)
Structures	541.0
Equipment (producer only)	128.0
Inventory (excluding monetary)	83.0
Total domestic stock	752.0
Net foreign assets	14.0
Total national stock in 1956	766.0

Kendrick's estimate for the domestic economy is for 1953 in 1929 prices.[2] In addition, structures include an adjustment of 39 per cent for land.[3] Excluding land from his estimate, we obtain an estimate of the 1953 stock in 1929 dollars as follows:

	(billion dollars)
Structures (excluding land)	210.2
Equipment (producer only)	87.0
Inventory (excluding monetary)	61.1
Total 1953 domestic stock in 1929 dollars	358.3

Kendrick does not have an estimate for this particular measure in 1957. However, he does present an estimate of stock for the entire domestic economy, including government and land. In 1953 these two components accounted for 27.6 per cent of this total, which was $494.9 billion. Using the same proportion to remove these items from his 1957 estimate of $559.3 billion to place it on a basis comparable to the Commerce data yields a domestic stock in 1957 of $404.9 billion in 1929 dollars. Adding $10.1 billion of net foreign assets yields total national stock in 1957 of $415.0 billion. To place this into 1947–9 dollars, we obtain from the Commerce estimates an implicit price index of capital which reveals that the ratio of 1947–9 prices to 1929 prices is 186.2:100. The total 1957 domestic stock in 1947–9 dollars is thus $772.5 billion.

Since United States capital stock grew at an average rate of 2 per cent per year over the period 1929–57, a rough estimate of the 1956 stock could be derived by reducing the 1957 estimate by 2 per cent. This gives us an estimate of United States capital stock of $757.4 billion in 1956.

BIBLIOGRAPHY, NOTES, INDEX

BIBLIOGRAPHY

Books

AITKEN, HUGH G. J. *American Capital and Canadian Resources.* Cambridge: Harvard University Press, 1961.

AITKEN, HUGH G. J. *et al. The American Economic Impact on Canada.* Duke University Commonwealth Studies Center, 12. Durham: Duke University Press, 1959.

BARNETT, HAROLD J. and MORSE, CHANDLER. *Scarcity and Growth: The Economics of National Resource Availability.* Recources for the Future, Inc. Baltimore: Johns Hopkins, 1963.

BJERKE, JUUL. "Some Aspects of Long-Term Economic Growth of Norway Since 1865." Study for the Sixth Conference of the International Association for Research in Income and Wealth, 1959. Unpublished.

BUCKLEY, KENNETH. *Capital Formation in Canada, 1896-1930.* Canadian Studies in Economics, 2. Toronto: University of Toronto Press, 1955.

CAVES, R. E. and HOLTON, R. H. *The Canadian Economy; Prospect and Retrospect.* Cambridge: Harvard University Press, 1959.

CLARK, COLIN. *The Conditions of Economic Progress.* London: St. Martin's Press, 1957.

CREAMER, D., DOBROVOLSKY, S. P., and BORENSTEIN, I. *Capital in Manufacturing and Mining.* National Bureau of Economic Research. Princeton: Princeton University Press, 1960.

DENISON, EDWARD F. *The Sources of Economic Growth in the United States and the Alternatives Before Us.* Supplementary Paper, 12. New York: Committee for Economic Development, 1962.

FIRESTONE, O. J. *Canada's Economic Development, 1867-1953.* Income and Wealth, Series VII. London: Bowes and Bowes, 1958.

——. *Residential Real Estate in Canada.* Toronto: University of Toronto Press, 1951.

GOLDSMITH, RAYMOND W. *The National Wealth of the United States in the Postwar Period.* National Bureau of Economic Research. Princeton: Princeton University Press, 1962.

GOLDSMITH, RAYMOND W. *et al. A Study of Saving in the United States.* 3 vols. Princeton: Princeton University Press, 1955 and 1956.

INNIS, HAROLD A. *Problems of Staple Production in Canada.* Toronto: Ryerson Press, 1933.

JOHANSEN, LEIF. *A Multi-Sectoral Study of Economic Growth.* Amsterdam: North Holland Publishing Company, 1960.

KENDRICK, JOHN W. *Productivity Trends in the United States.* National Bureau of Economic Research. Princeton: Princeton University Press, 1961.

KUZNETS, SIMON. *Capital in the American Economy: Its Formation and Financing.* National Bureau of Economic Research. Princeton: Princeton University Press, 1961.

PODOLUK, J. R. *Earnings and Education.* Ottawa: Dominion Bureau of Statistics, 1965.

STOVEL, JOHN A. *Canada in the World Economy.* Cambridge: Harvard University Press, 1959.

ULMER, MELVILLE J. *Capital in Transportation, Communications, and Public Utilities.* National Bureau of Economic Research. Princeton: Princeton University Press, 1960.

Articles

ABRAMOVITZ, MOSES. "Economic Growth in the United States," *American Economic Review,* Sept. 1962.

CAVES, R. E. "The Inter-Industry Study of the Canadian Economy," *Canadian Journal of Economics and Political Science,* Aug. 1957.

——. "Vent for Surplus: Model of Trade and Growth," in *Trade, Growth and the Balance of Payments.* Chicago: Rand McNally, 1965.

DOMAR, EVSEY D. "On Total Productivity and All That," *Journal of Political Economy,* Dec. 1962.

HOUTHAKKER, H. S. "Education and Income," *Review of Economics and Statistics,* Feb. 1959.

KRAVIS, I. B. "Relative Income Shares in Fact and Theory," *American Economic Review,* Dec. 1959.

KUZNETS, SIMON. "Quantitative Aspects of the Economic Growth of Nations." IV. "Distributions of National Income by Factor Shares," *Economic Development and Cultural Change*, VII, 3, part II, April 1959. VI. "Long Term Trends in Capital Formation Proportions," *Economic Development and Cultural Change*, IX, 4, part II, July 1961.

MINCER, JACOB. "On-the-Job Training; Costs, Returns and Some Implications," *Journal of Political Economy*, Supplement on Investment in Human Beings, Oct. 1962.

PENTLAND, H. C. "Physical Productivity in Canada, 1935-1952," *Economic Journal*, June 1954.

SCHULTZ, THEODORE W. "Reflections on Investment in Man," *Journal of Political Economy*, Supplement on Investment in Human Beings, Oct. 1962.

SOLOW, R. "Technical Change and the Aggregate Production Function," *Review of Economics and Statistics*, Aug. 1957.

WATKINS, MELVILLE H. "A Staple Theory of Economic Growth," *Canadian Journal of Economics and Political Science*, May 1963.

GOVERNMENT OF CANADA PUBLICATIONS

Department of Labour. *Changes in the Occupational Composition of the Canadian Labour Force 1931-61*, by Noah M. Meltz. Occasional Paper No. 2. Ottawa, 1965.

—— . *The Migration of Professional Workers into and out of Canada*. Professional Manpower Bulletin, 11. Ottawa, 1961.

——. *Wages and Hours of Labour in Canada*. Ottawa, annually.

Department of Trade and Commerce. *Private and Public Investment in Canada, 1926-1951*. Ottawa, 1951.

Dominion Bureau of Statistics. *Annual Supplement to the Monthly Index of Industrial Production*. Ottawa, 1966.

——. *Canada's International Investment Position, 1926-1954*. Ottawa, 1957.

——. *Canada Year Book*. Ottawa, 1961, 1926, 1957-8.

——. *The Canadian Balance of International Payments, 1960, and International Investment Position*. Ottawa, 1962 (1958).

Canadian Labour Force Estimates, 1931-1945. Reference paper 23. Ottawa, 1957.

——. *Canadian Statistical Review*, 1959 and 1961 Supplements. Ottawa, 1960, 1962.

——. *Employment and Payrolls*. Annually.

——. *Estimates of Fixed Capital Flows and Stocks Manufacturing Canada 1926-60*, Ottawa, 1965.

Index of Industrial Production, 1935-1957, Reference Paper 34. Ottawa, 1959.

——. *Indexes of Real Domestic Product by Industry of Origin, 1935-1961*. Ottawa, 1963.

——. *The Inter-industry Flow of Goods and Services, 1949*. Supplement to Reference Paper 72. Ottawa, 1959.

Man-hours and Hourly Earnings. Annually.

National Accounts: Income and Expenditure, 1926-1956. Ottawa, 1958.

——. *Preliminary Statistics of Education, 1961-62*. Ottawa, 1962.

——. *Prices and Price Indexes, 1913-32*. Ottawa, 1934.

——. *Private and Public Investment in Canada, 1946-1957*. Ottawa, 1959.

——. *Statistical Yearbook of Canada, 1900*. Ottawa.

Economic Council of Canada. *Second Annual Review: Towards Sustained and Balanced Economic Growth*. Ottawa, 1965.

——. *Immigration and Emigration of Professional and Skilled Manpower During the Post-war Period*, by Louis Parai. Special Study 1. Ottawa, 1965.

Bank of Canada. *Statistical Summary Supplement*. Ottawa, 1961.

Senate of Canada. Special Committee on Manpower and Employment. *Proceedings*. 1. Nov. 1960.

Royal Commission on Canada's Economic Prospects. *Output, Labour and Capital in the Canadian Economy*, by W. C. Hood and A. Scott. Ottawa, 1957.

——. *Canada-United States Economic Relations*, by I. Brecher and S. S. Reisman. Ottawa, 1957.

UNITED STATES GOVERNMENT PUBLICATIONS

Department of Commerce. *Historical Statistics of the United States, Colonial Times to 1957*. Washington, 1960.

——. *Income and Output*. Washington, 1958.

——. *Survey of Current Business*, Oct., Nov., 1962.

Economic Report of the President. Washington, 1957.

NOTES

CHAPTER ONE

1. The key users of this tool are Denison, Domar, Kendrick, and Solow, whose works are listed in the bibliography.

CHAPTER TWO

1. Often capital is defined to include land.
2. Edward F. Denison, *The Sources of Economic Growth in the United States and the Alternatives Before Us* (New York, 1962).
3. Canada, Dominion Bureau of Statistics, *Canadian Labour-Force Estimates, 1931-1945* (Ottawa, 1957), 20, for 1926 figures; *idem, Canadian Statistical Review* (Ottawa, 1960), 1, for 1956 figures.
4. Real GNE is given in DBS, *National Accounts: Income and Expenditure, 1926-1956* (Ottawa, 1958), 36; *1961*, 58.
5. *Economic Report of the President* (Washington, 1957), 127.

CHAPTER THREE

1. DBS, *Canadian Statistical Review* (Ottawa, 1960), 7, Table 4.
2. The main elements in this rapid population increase have been migration and natural increase. Over the period, net migration contributed directly only 13.3 per cent of the total increase, leaving natural increase, which includes the children born to migrants in Canada, as a key factor. In the period 1925-9, Canada's birth rate was 24.2 per thousand of population, its death rate was 11.2, and the rate of natural increase was, therefore, 13.0. By 1956, the birth rate had increased to 28.0, the death rate was cut to 8.2, and the rate of natural increase rose to 19.8, one of the highest in the developed world.
3. DBS, *Canadian Statistical Review*, 35, Table 8.
4. US Dept. of Commerce, *Historical Statistics of the United States, Colonial Times to 1957* (Washington, 1960), Series D1-12, 70. The concept in the US is slightly different from the Canadian; the latter considers the proportion of the civilian non-institutional population in the labour force, and the former includes, in the population figure, the persons in institutions, and includes members of the armed forces in the labour force.
5. For a further discussion of the elements responsible for the observed trend in participation rates, see the study paper by T. Wilson and N. H. Lithwick for the Royal Commission on Taxation, *Taxation and Economic Growth*, forthcoming.
6. Moses Abramovitz, "Economic Growth in the United States," *American Economic Review*, LII (Sept. 1962), 762.
7. Denison, *The Sources of Economic Growth*, 81, Table 10.
8. Other elements, such as on-the-job instruction, adult education, and the like, enter into the training of the labour force. As yet, these are difficult to quantify, but their importance should not be overlooked. A pathbreaking analysis is provided by Jacob Mincer in his paper "On-the-Job Training: Costs, Returns, and Some Implications," *Journal of Political Economy*, Supplement on Investment in Human Beings, LXX (Oct. 1962), 50.
9. Denison, *The Sources of Economic Growth*, 72, Table 9 (1).
10. Abramovitz, "Economic Growth in the United States." 762.
11. Theodore W. Schultz, "Reflections on Investment in Man," *Journal of Political Economy*, Supplement (Oct. 1962), LXX, 6, Table 1 in particular.
12. William C. Hood and Anthony Scott, *Output, Labour and Capital in the Canadian Economy, Royal Commission on Canada's Economic Prospects* (Ottawa, 1957), 451, Table 6B. 7.
13. See Table A-5 for an indication of the discrepancy involved.
14. An article by Melville H. Watkins, "A Staple Theory of Economic Growth," gives a review of much of the literature on the staple theory. *Canadian Journal of Economics and*

Political Science (May, 1963). See also Richard E. Caves, "Vent for Surplus: Model of Trade and Growth," in *Trade, Growth and the Balance of Payments* (Chicago, 1965).

15. This differs from what we would ideally desire because the discovery of resources is one step removed from their flow into the productive system.

16. A book of considerable interest in this regard is Harold J. Barnett and Chandler Morse, *Scarcity and Growth: The Economics of Natural Resource Availability* (Baltimore, 1963).

17. Simon Kuznets, "Quantitative Aspects of the Economic Growth of Nations." IV. "Distribution of National Income by Factor Shares," *Economic Development and Cultural Change*, VII, no. 3, part II (April 1959), 23-8.

18. This corresponds to "economy-wide" allocation in I. B. Kravis. "Relative Income Shares in Fact and Theory," *American Economic Review*, XLIX (Dec. 1959), 917-47.

19. DBS, *The Inter-industry Flow of Goods and Services, 1949*, Supplement to reference paper no. 72 (Ottawa, 1959).

20. O. J. Firestone, *Canada's Economic Development 1867-1953* (London, 1958), Tables 99 and 100.

21. See Appendix G for a more comprehensive discussion of the role of foreigners.

22. Denison, *The Sources of Economic Growth*, 266, Table 32. He compares his findings to those of Kendrick in chapter 14.

23. See Table 6.

24. This is because of the great improvement in the quality of the United States labour force, as we have indicated in Table 6.

25. See Table 1.

CHAPTER FOUR

1. L. A. Johansen, *A Multi-Sectoral Study of Economic Growth* (Amsterdam. 1960), 74-6. The author derives his factor coefficients by the use of factor shares in national income also.

2. These procedures are described in DBS, reference paper 34, *Index of Industrial Production*, and the 1959 revision thereof. Data in this paper cover only mining manufacturing and electric power and gas utilities which accounted for just 32 per cent of GDP in 1949. The reference paper, *Real Domestic Product by Industry of Origin, 1935-61* (Ottawa, 1963) has extended these estimates to cover the rest of the economy. DBS published major revisions to its Index of constant dollar GDP in May 1966 (DBS-61-005 *Annual Supplement to the Monthly Index of Industrial Production*). These revisions have primarily affected manufacturing, and. in particular, several of its major groups. We *have* included the revised data in the text. and present a comparison of these with the unrevised data in Appendix H. A more detailed analysis of these revisions by major groups in manufacturing is presented in a paper by N. H. Lithwick, with George Post and T. K. Rymes, "Postwar Production Relationships in Canada," to be published winter 1966 by the National Bureau of Economic Research in its *Conference on Postwar Production Relations*.

3. The percentage unemployed was 9.1 in 1937 and 7.2 in 1961. DBS, *Canadian Statistical Review*, Table 1.

4. See Table 4, DBS, *National Accounts*, for the relationship of GNP to GDP. Also, Hood and Scott, *Output, Labour and Capital*, chap. 5, Appendix D, 357-74.

5. See Table 10B.

6. DBS, *The Inter-Industry Flow of Goods and Services*, Table 1.

7. This is done for the years 1937, 1949, and 1961 in Table B-16.

8. Our aggregates are determined by arithmetically combining the components. The theoretically correct method is a geometric combination, such as is given in Table 27. The differences, however, are slight, and we prefer to retain the generally understood concepts. See Appendix F for further discussion.

9. John W. Kendrick, *Productivity Trends in the United States* (Princeton. 1961), 64-5.

10. An exploratory work in this area is Jacob Mincer's "On-the-Job Training: Costs, Returns, and some Implications," *Journal of Political Economy*, LXX (Oct. 1962), S129.

CHAPTER FIVE

1. Denison's growth rates are: Output, 2.93 per cent; Labour (on our concept) 1.20 per cent; Capital, 1.88 per cent. Man-hours alone in government and the military grew by 3.96 per cent (Kendrick, *Productivity Trends in the United States*, 314-15, Table A-XI). This explains the difference between the growth of labour input on the national as compared to the private domestic basis.

2. Tables 34 and 21 respectively.

3. For Canada, see Table 19.

4. The attractiveness of Canadian mineral resources has been the main factor on the demand side leading to this shift on an international basis.

5. Lithwick, Post and Rymes, "Postwar Production Relationships in Canada," to be published in the NBER's *Conference on Production Relations* late in 1966. See also chap. 6 n. 4.

CHAPTER SIX

1. Their derivation is described in Appendix E.

2. Education is broadly defined here to include on-the-job training and similar non-formal types of improvement.

3. Kendrick, *Productivity Trends in the United States*, 285, Table A-10. For the three periods, the labour term is 0.64, 0.68, and 0.77.

4. Juul Bjerke, *Some Aspects of Long-Term Economic Growth of Norway Since 1865*, a paper presented to the Sixth Conference of the International Association for Research in Income and Wealth, September, 1959. See 27, Table IV.1.

5. *Ibid.*, 40.

6. Simon Kuznets, "Quantitative Aspects of the Economic Growth of Nations," VI. Long-Term Trends in Capital Formation Proportions, *Economic Development and Cultural Change* (July 1961), 80, Table N-1. The ratio used is GDCF/GDP.

7. *Ibid.*, GNCF/GNP, 92, Table US-1.

8. *Ibid.*, GDCF/GDP, 102, Table C-1.

CHAPTER SEVEN

1. This new chapter is adapted from the author's publication *Prices, Productivity, and Canada's Competitive Position* (Montreal, 1967), with the kind permission of the Private Planning Association of Canada.

2. See Economic Council of Canada, *Third Annual Review*, or the Governor's 1966 *Report* for the Bank of Canada, 3.

3. In the model

$$Y = AL^aK^b$$

we shall assume constant returns to scale, so that $a + b = 1$, or $b = 1 - a$. If we assume that the factors are paid their marginal products, then we can solve the equation for A, the level of technology, and compare this as between the two countries. See also note 9.

4. See appendix I for a full description of these estimates.

5. Appendix A, 81.

6. T. M. Brown, *Canadian Economic Growth*, Study for the Royal Commission on Health Services, Table B-1, 198–9.

7. Edward F. Denison, *The Sources of Economic Growth in the United States and The Alternatives Before Us*, Supplementary Paper no. 13, Committee for Economic Development (Jan. 1962), Table 4, 80.

8. Table 11, 18.

9. It might be argued that the assumption of a homogeneous production function required for the use of this type of analysis is likely to be violated in a cross-sectional comparison. Intuitively one would expect that production functions in two countries would have vastly different shapes, violating the assumption of homogeneity. I would argue, however, that Canada in 1956 would be more like the United States in that year than was the United States thirty years prior. Since most growth studies make the homogeneity assumption for the latter situation, our technique is much less heroic than appears at first blush.

10. This touches on the important theoretical problem raised by Joan Robinson with respect to the bias of conventional capital-stock measures because they include technical improvements. A variant of the *real*-capital concept which would remove the efficiency factor from the stocks would be an interesting extension of the present discussion.

11. Weighting the United States and Canadian populations according to their educational attainments in 1965 by the average return to these various levels of education reveals that the United States population's income was 7.5 per cent higher as a result of its much greater level of education, particularly at the senior levels. 52.1 per cent of the population over eighteen completed high school or better, whereas in Canada the proportion was only 25.9 per cent. This accounts for one-fourth of our measured productivity gap of 29 per cent. DBS, *Educational Attainment of the Canadian Population and Labour Force*, 1960-5, Special Labour Force Studies no. 1 (1966), Table 15, 18.

12. Tables 19 and 34, 25 and 38 respectively.

13. Economic Council, *Third Annual Review*, Chart 6-61, 212.

14. Calculated from $4.7 = \check{A}_{us} + 0.77 (1.0) + 0.23 (1.6)$.

15. Calculated from $5.0 = A_c + 0.77 (1.5) + 0.23 (3.5)$.

16.   N. H. Lithwick, *Science Policy in Canada and the Economy* (Toronto, 1969).
17.   Table 59, page 59.
18.   DBS, *National Accounts, Income and Expenditure* (Ottawa), various issues.
19.   8.4 per cent versus 6.7 per cent in current dollars, and 3.8 per cent versus 1.7 per cent in constant dollars.
20.   4.5 per cent versus 4.1 per cent in current dollars, and 2.2 per cent versus 1.8 per cent in constant dollars.
21.   This excludes income of unincorporated enterprises.
22.   This argument is reinforced by the fact that although there has been a substantial increase in net migration into Canada (increased immigration *and* reduced emigration), Canada has been able to reduce its unemployment rate.
23.   Devaluation could offset these macro effects, as could a floating exchange rate. These do not appear to be acceptable alternatives to the government, however.
24.   These points apply with equal vigour to professional and rentier income. Our emphasis on labour is due primarily to the explicit adoption of this goal by some of its leaders.
25.   While the pieces of evidence on the sources of growth have begun to accumulate, there is little evidence of a willingness to adopt a growth policy with the strategy clearly delineated. Our present chaotic rush into public-school construction and shotgun research grants shows no foundation in a *rational* growth program.

CHAPTER EIGHT

1.   Denison, *The Sources of Economic Growth*.
2.   Table A-5.
3.   Tables A-1 through A-4 for the economy, and Tables B-1 through B-11 for the industrial estimates.
4.   The recent publication of capital stock series for manufacturing by DBS enabled the calculation of inter-industry shifts within Canadian manufacturing. See DBS, *Estimates of Fixed Capital, Flows and Stocks, Manufacturing, Canada, 1916-1960*, 1965.
5.   See Table 6 for the role of the various quality items.
6.   See Table 8.
7.   Appendix G contains further indications of the role of the United States in this connection.

APPENDIX A

1.   K. Buckley, *Capital Formation in Canada, 1896-1930*, Canadian Studies in Economics No. 2 (Toronto, 1955).
2.   O. J. Firestone, *Canada's Economic Development, 1867-1953*, Income and Wealth, Series VII (London, 1958).
3.   Hood and Scott, *Output, Labour and Capital*, chap. 6.
4.   Excludes residential construction under Veterans' Land Act. Veterans' rental housing constructed by Central Mortgage and Housing Corp. and joint federal-provincial housing.
5.   Firestone, *Canada's Economic Development*, 85, Table 19.
6.   Buckley, *Capital Formation in Canada*, 139, Table N.
7.   *Ibid.*, 128, Table A-2.
8.   DBS, *National Accounts, Income and Expenditure, 1926-1956*, and later editions, Table 2 line 6, Table 54 line 2; Price Index, Table 6 line 6.
9.   Hood and Scott, *Output, Labour and Capital*, Series 7809, 487 (7).
10.   DBS, *Private and Public Investment in Canada, 1946-1957* (Ottawa, 1959), 12 (2).
11.   Buckley, *Capital Formation in Canada*, 130, Table C. Brought to market prices, 132, Table D.
12.   DBS, *Prices and Price Indexes, 1913-1932* (Ottawa, 1934), 16, Table III.
13.   Hood and Scott, *Output, Labour and Capital*, 473-86 (8).
14.   Firestone, *Canada's Economic Development*, 101, Table 30.
15.   *Ibid.*, 276, Table 87.
16.   *Ibid.*, 100, Tables 29 and 30. Between 1870 and 1890, current dollar gross investment as a percentage of current dollar GNE rose from 11.8 to 13.9. In constant dollars, this ratio increased from 13.1 to 15.2.
17.   Buckley, *Capital Formation in Canada*, 129.
18.   *Ibid.*, 128, Table A-2.
19.   DBS, *National Accounts, 1926-1956*, 36-7, Table 5, line 7.
20.   DBS, *Statistical Yearbook of Canada, 1900*, 455.
21.   Buckley, *Capital Formation in Canada*, 138, Table L and 139, Table M, distributed to an annual basis by Table A-2.

22. Hood and Scott, *Output, Labour and Capital*, Series 7002, 445, Table 6B.4.

23. *Ibid.*, 234-7.

24. Buckley, *Capital Formation in Canada*, 133, Table F.

25. DBS, *Prices and Price Indexes, 1913-1932*, 15, Table I.

26. This is obtained by dividing the change in inventories in constant (1949) dollars for the year 1926 into the current dollar value of the change in inventories for the same year, DBS, *National Accounts, 1926-1956*, Table 2 and Table 5.

27. Buckley, *Capital Formation in Canada*, 133, Table E.

28. DBS, *National Accounts*, Table 5.

29. DBS, *Canada's International Investment Position, 1926-54*, 73, Table III. Bank of Canada, *Statistical Summary*, Supplement (Ottawa, 1961), 147.

30. Excludes foreign investment in Canadian government bonds, which are taken to be non-productive debt in the national accounts framework.

31. H. S. Houthakker, "Education and Income," *Review of Economics and Statistics* (Feb. 1959), 25.

32. DBS, *Preliminary Statistics of Education, 1961-62*, 50, Table 35, and J. R. Podoluk, *Earnings and Education* (DBS, 1965), 21, Table 6.

33. DBS, *Canada Year Book, 1961*, 184, Table 1; 195, Table 11.

34. An interesting related document has been published by the Department of Labour entitled *The Migration of Professional Workers into and out of Canada, 1946-1960*, Professional Manpower Bulletin No. 11 (Ottawa, 1961). Some idea of Canada's net gain or loss of "educational capital" through migration would be a particularly useful addition to our understanding of growth.

35. DBS, *National Accounts, 1926-1956*, 27.

36. *Ibid.*, 34-5, Table 4.

37. *Ibid.*, 96-7, Table 52.

38. Firestone, *Canada's Economic Development*, Table 99.

39. Hood and Scott, *Output, Labour and Capital*, 425, Table 6B2.

40. Firestone, *Canada's Economic Development*, Table 100.

APPENDIX B

1. Firestone, *Canada's Economic Development*, 306, Table 93, adjusted to the end of the calendar year.

2. Table A-5.

APPENDIX C

1. John W. Kendrick, *Productivity Trends in the United States* (Princeton, 1961).

2. US Dept. of Commerce, *Survey of Current Business* (October 1962), 9. Table 1.

3. Kendrick, *Productivity Trends in the United States*, 314, Table A-XI.

4. Houthakker, "Education and Income," *Review of Economics and Statistics* (Feb. 1959), 163, n. 31. These differentials are adjusted for the rent component following Denison, *The Sources of Economic Growth*, 68 (2).

5. The sources of these data are: For 1950, Census of Population, 1950, Vol. IV, Special Report P-E no. 5B, *Education*, 5B-88, Table 11. Conversion from occupations to industries classification based on same census, Special Report P-E no. 1D, 34, Table 6. For 1940, Bureau of the Census, *Population; Education*, from the 1940 Census of Population, 1947, 103, Table 21. Conversion based on Census of Population, 1940, *Labour Force (Sample Statistics)*, Industrial Characteristics, 137, Table 11.

6. Kendrick, *Productivity Trends in the United States*, 367, Table B-III.

7. US Dept. of Commerce, *Survey of Current Business* (Nov. 1962), 15, Table 4. We have used the "Bulletin F" lives for the net stock estimate, assuming straight line depreciation.

8. Kendrick, *Productivity Trends in the United States*, 464, Table D-I.

9. *Ibid.*, 394, Table C-21.

10. US Dept. of Commerce, *Income and Output*, 193, Table V-7.

11. *Ibid.*, 220, Table VII-2.

12. Simon Kuznets, *Capital in the American Economy: Its Formation and Financing* (Princeton, 1961), 492, Table R-5.

13. Raymond W. Goldsmith, *The National Wealth of the United States in the Postwar Period* (New York, 1962), 77, Table 17.

14. Melville J. Ulmer, *Capital in Transportation, Communications and Public Utilities* (New York, 1960).

APPENDIX D

1. Kendrick, *Productivity Trends in the United States,* 488, Table D-VIII.
2. *Ibid.,* 468-75.
3. Goldsmith, *The National Wealth of the United States in the Postwar Period,* 76, Table 16.
4. Kendrick, *Productivity Trends in the United States,* 453, Table D-13.

APPENDIX E

1. Kendrick, *Productivity Trends in the United States,* 314, Table A-XI.
2. Denison, *The Sources of Economic Growth,* 72, Table 9 (1).
3. Calculated as $6.1 + (14.2 \times 28/30)$.
4. Denison, *The Sources of Economic Growth,* 81, Table 10 (1). Calculated as 1.24/2.14.
5. *Ibid.,* 72, Table 9 (1). The ratio is $(2.7 \times 2.7)/4.4$.
6. Kendrick, *Productivity Trends in the United States,* 285, Table A-10 (3) and (4).
7. *Ibid.,* 358, Table B-2; 395, Table C-23; 453, Table D-14; and the weighted components of Appendices G and H.

APPENDIX F

1. For a more technical discussion of this problem, see the paper by Evsey D. Domar, "On Total Productivity and All That," in *Journal of Political Economy* (Dec. 1962), 597.

APPENDIX G

1. Since imports with the exception of capital goods do not constitute primary inputs, they do not enter into our production function. Similarly exports, being a component of final demand which we do not explicitly investigate, do not fit into our analysis. The difference between exports and imports consists of capital flows, the long term components thereof being a very important element in our model. These latter will be considered in some detail subsequently.
2. DBS, *Canadian Statistical Review,* 1959 Supplement, 125, Table 50, and 129, Table 51. 1961, 58, Table 80, and 60, Table 81.
The separate deflation of imports and exports as we have done here may lead to a residual "real" balance of trade differing in sign from the current dollar term. The conceptual problem thereby posed is inherent in the subtraction of deflated data, and there is little one can do to resolve it save use the relevant measures where applicable. Thus, the use of deflated exports and imports is meaningful when referring to the disposition of real output, and use of the current dollar balance deflated by an appropriate price index when considering the financial implications of trade.
This same problem arises in production indexes such as we have been using. In these, base year net output is projected by subtracting constant dollar material, fuel, and electricity inputs from constant dollar output. This procedure is used because of the inability to deflate value added in any other manner, rather than for theoretically sound reasons. As a result, a number of expedients have been adopted to improve the quality of this measure, and those are described in the DBS reference paper, *Revised Index of Industrial Production,* 935-57, 9-35.
3. Hugh G. J. Aitken, in his comprehensive study of the role of US capital in Canadian economic development, concludes that "it is clear that the contribution of foreign capital to Canadian capital formation in recent years has been large, and that it has been growing larger." *American Capital and Canadian Resources* (Cambridge, 1961), 62.

APPENDIX H

1. Lithwick, Post and Rymes, "Postwar Production Relationships," contains an analysis of the effect of these revisions on the major groups within manufacturing.
2. Economic Council, *Second Annual Review,* 33-5, 18, Table 2-4.

APPENDIX I

1. United States Department of Commerce, *The Statistical History of the United States,* combined edition including *Continuation to 1962 and Revisions* (Stamford, 1965), 152.
2. J. Kendrick, *Productivity Trends in the United States* (Princeton, 1961), 322–5.
3. *Ibid.,* 276.

INDEX

Lightning Source UK Ltd.
Milton Keynes UK
UKHW030613210722
406167UK00006B/660